Larry,
Thanks for ev[erything]
Stay "Cool"

Jewett

(916) 968-0844

A Ghostly Reign Of Terror

iN tHE cAR

A Ghostly Reign Of Terror

iN tHE cAR

By:

Lonnie Faustino DeWitt

RLD Enterprise

Copyright © 1996 by Lonnie Faustino DeWitt

All rights reserved. No part of this book may be reproduced or transmitted in any form or by any means, electronic or mechanical, including photocopying, recording, or by any information storage and retrieval system, without permission, in writing, from the publisher.

Published by RLD Enterprise, Post Office Box 22765, Sacramento, CA 95822-0765.

Autographed copies of *iN tHE cAR* may be requested by writing the author at P.O. Box 22765, Sacramento, CA 95822. Checks/money orders should be made payable to RLD Enterprise. The above address may also be used when requesting the author for speaking engagements or, you may call (916) I-C-AGAIN (or, I-C-A-GAIN) (916) 422-4246. Web Page: http://www.gvn.net/~inthecar/ E-Mail: inthecar@gvn.net

Manufactured in the United States of America.

Front Cover Design by Lonnie F. DeWitt.

Front Cover Illustration by Brother Isaac Pearson and Mr. Neill Brengettsey.

Rear Cover Photograph of author taken on October 4, 1997, commemorating his 32nd year Polytechnic High School Class Reunion. Photograph courtesy of Campus Candids, P.O. Box 1485, Davis, CA 95617.

Chapters 1, 4, 7, 8, 9, 10, 11, 13, 14, 15, 17, 18 and 19 Illustrations by Mr. Neill Brengettsey.

Chapters 5 and 16 Illustrations by Brother Isaac Pearson.

ISBN 0-9657816-0-7

10 9 8 7 6 5 4 3 2

First Edition

Contents

Acknowledgments	ix
Dedication	1
Preface	3
Chapter 1 - When The Car Crashes	7
Chapter 2 - The Valley	17
Chapter 3 - Class of '65	23
Chapter 4 - A Great Way of Life	29
Chapter 5 - Men, Women and Colored	41
Chapter 6 - Ambassador in Blue	47
Chapter 7 - An Arrogant, Smart-ass, You-Know-What	55
Chapter 8 - R-e-s-p-e-c-t	61
Chapter 9 - A Volley of Set-ups	69
Chapter 10 - Professionally Unprofessional	81
Chapter 11 - Forbidden Friendship	95
Chapter 12 - Ruthie	105
Chapter 13 - Against My Objections	111
Chapter 14 - Buzzards vs. Vultures	129
Chapter 15 - The Olympian Set-up (The Mother of All Set-ups)	143
Chapter 16 - Conspiracy of Silence	157
Chapter 17 - Master of Illusions	179
Chapter 18 - Beyond the Pain	189
Chapter 19 - The Afterbirth	195
Ode to The Dynamic Trio	209
About the Author	211

Acknowledgments

My God who gave me the torch that I may clearly see my vision and purpose in this transient life. **He** blessed me with dignity, character and other personal attributes to help me make a meaningful contribution to mankind.

My wife, Ruthie, and our immediate families who felt my agonizing pain and believed in me. Their many prayers and unyielding words of comfort helped me to overcome and look beyond my own personal trauma. I will forever be indebted to their thoughtfulness and sincerity.

My mom, Alice, who taught me the importance of human values: love, honor, respect, kindness and the unselfish giving of oneself. She instilled in me the concepts of fairness and the priceless fundamental to my own self-worth - integrity. My mom will forever remain an inseparable part of my life.

My friends, associates and other family members who I trusted to offer me constructive criticism as I wrote and rewrote my manuscript more often than I care to remember. Special thanks to my two sons, Kenslo and Lonnie, Jr., who both proofread my manuscript to help ease my *shoe string* budget. Thanks are also extended to Lori Black, Eva Weston Brown, Tamara Gary-EL, Boyd P. Lane, JoAnne Belizare-Lewis, Gwen and Terri Mason, Gale Moore, Jim Morales, Beverly Reeves, Tanya Robinson, Elizabeth Proctor, Rayfield L. Scott, Anita Thrower, Patricia Wilson and a host of others who shared with me the benefit of their experiences, their valuable time and their endless words of encouragement. My most deepest gratitude is also given to Brother Isaac Pearson and Mr. Neill Brengettsey, my artistic illustrators.

Lastly, I wish to *acknowledge* the California Department of Corrections, the California Correctional Peace Officers Association and the California State Personnel Board. Without each of them, this book would not have been possible.

DEDICATION

Alice, my beloved mother. I'll forever cherish the sweet and fond memories that we shared. You taught me character and love - for that, and much more, I thank you.

I dedicate this book to all people of Color. I pray that regardless of our *status* in life, each of us will show respect and dignity toward one another; and not be tempted to humor White America by disrespecting our common bond - our heritage. Further, I caution and beg each of us to deny others from crossing that line.

Special dedication and gratitude are given to my wife, Ruthie, who has been my inspirational cornerstone and pillars of strength, trust, devotion, and unwavering love. Ruthie continues to show courage, determination and tolerance while coping with my aggravated mood swings precipitated by my sudden and long-term unemployment.

Lastly, I dedicate *iN tHE cAR* to my three children, Kenslo, Lonnie Jr., and Shaneé; and to all children and young adults who are destined, by virtue of their color, to pick up and carry the torch for future generations to follow.

Enough *is* **enough**! The *aisle* that leads to self-respect demands our continued and unwavering vigilance.

Lonnie

PREFACE

Within the California Department of Corrections, the term *iN tHE cAR* epitomizes this make-believe vehicle as the optimal and most progressive mode of transportation for one's upward mobility. For one to be referred as being *iN tHE cAR*, therefore, makes a very strong and undeniable statement that the individual is *protected* by management and it is explicitly understood that the individual is *somebody's kid* who can do no wrong (in the eyesight of correctional staff). This myth is endorsed and perpetuated by CDC management while giving credence to those token-riding passengers.

Therefore, for one to be *iN tHE cAR* **boldly** entitles that member to receive the best of assignments and the best watch (hours) which generally means *real* weekends off. While there are exceptions, the great majority of these individuals enjoy their comfortable lifestyles *iN tHE cAR* only after they have demonstrated a sincere tolerance to boot-licking and ass-kissing.

iN tHE cAR will **not** attempt to address the somewhat *customary* - yet, quite illicit - sexual acts performed by both driver and occupants who wish to remain in their respective positions.

This book will, however, express my sentiments, grievances, insights, experiences, and frustrations that I encountered as a correctional officer at Folsom State Prison (FSP - old Folsom), California State Prison (CSP - new Folsom); and as a State parole agent assigned to the Race Street, San Jose Parole Office.

iN tHE cAR will explore the California Department of Corrections and its flagrant yet consistent mismanagement. Furthermore, *iN tHE cAR* will address how these wannabe managers attempt to manage their employees through fear and intimidation.

In my opinion, these managers use the old **who-you-know-who-you-owe-who-you-blow** concept to determine upward mobility and *ideal* job placements.

If it weren't so sad, it would be humorous for one to observe the metamorphic transformation of one of these good ole boys (and gals) who were previously *one of us* now, magically, turns into *one of them* (Blacks included).

There is, however, a commonality among each of *them* since most develop a streak extending from the upper part of the neck to the lower part of the tail bone (most commonly referred to as a *yellow streak*)! The majority find it much easier (and certainly less threatening) to walk a well-beaten path.

The late Dr. Martin Luther King, Jr., once said:

"The ultimate measure of a man is not where he stands in moments of comfort and convenience, but where he stands at times of challenge and controversy."

It's common knowledge throughout the State of California that CDC management goes to great extremes to *avoid* both challenge and controversy.

The California Department of Corrections reeks with nepotism and the good ole boy (and gal) *promote me concept*. Within this System, there exists - what I will label as our *vultures* - an appreciative number of *wannabes*. With very few exceptions, the majority of these *wannabes* are determined to do whatever is necessary - legal and/or illegal, moral and/or immoral - to achieve their desired goal. That goal is, of course, to either get *iN tHE cAR* or remain therein.

iN tHE cAR will give the reader a look inside two State penal institutions (Folsom State Prison and California State Prison) that lack integrity and reek with corruption.

There exists a total lack of sensitivity, benign indifference and neglect on part of management. It matters not whether the issues involve a convicted felon or a staff member who, invariably, will be a minority and **not** *iN tHE cAR*.

Finally, this book will share some insight into the paradox that minority peace officers (and in fact Black Americans) face daily in our attempts to *fit* into Corporate America while trying to maintain our individualism and cultural autonomy.

Unfortunately, these institutional (wannabe) power brokers remind us daily that the *glass ceiling* is very real and that our success (or failure) in attempting to climb the corporate ladder (especially, within the California Department of Corrections) depends entirely on these *institutional(ized) corporate maggots* and their subjective views and/or support (or, lack thereof) toward us both individually (as a person) and collectively (as a people).

It should, therefore, come as no surprise for us to know that few Black men's voices speak loud enough to be heard over the political rhetoric and oftentimes hidden agendas of *White Corrections*.

My negative and painful experiences within the California Department of Corrections have simply strengthened my resolve to help identify and possibly eradicate some of the socio-political inequities facing Black peace officers and other minority staff. By design, this *targeted group* has, therefore, become daily victims of serious and painfully obvious administrative and legal deficiencies while suffering from gross and flagrant misrepresentation and under-representation.

Chapter One

When the Car Crashes

I found out early on that I was simply just out of place in this System - this System of immorality; this unethical system; this System that bears no allegiance, no loyalty; this System that appears to be self-serving and offers few rewards to its minority staff.

I was equivalent to that proverbial square peg desperately trying to fit into a round hole - it just couldn't happen; I simply could not fit.

I sincerely wanted to be a Parole Agent because of my education and vast managerial skills, experiences and travels. I really believed that I could make a difference. I still believe that I could have made a meaningful difference in the lives of the parolees on my caseload, their families, and the community, had the CDC System *allowed* me.

Unfortunately, it appeared that the CDC *image* of its Black employee was that of a *head bowing, foot shuffling, "we sick, boss?" spook!* CDC obviously had me confused with that *other guy* (who you will later meet). I offer no apologies; I was simply not the one.

The negative images that the news media have projected toward Black Americans are ludicrous. Admittedly, the negative images that *some* Black Americans have shown to help perpetuate those myths are equally disgusting.

Nonetheless, please believe that *not* every Black man with a gun is your enemy and every White man with a badge is *clearly not* your friend. As it is in the institution, everyone in blue denims (the customary attire for inmates) is not necessarily the enemy; and everyone in green (staff uniform) is not necessarily your friend.

It's interesting for one to observe the psychological behaviors that manifest themselves in the driver and passengers *when the car crashes*. The art of ass kissing then becomes not too distasteful (since *most* of the car occupants have previously gone that *route*). They will quickly build yet another car and eliminate some of the **undesirables** who previously sat (very comfortably) in the crashed vehicle. Almost always, one of the undesirables would certainly be the previous driver, whose sudden (or gradual demise) resulted from his or her becoming a victim of a political drive-by (similar to the political commotion that *iN tHE cAR* will, undoubtedly, stir).

Political correctness is the buzzword within the California Department of Corrections. It's just not good enough for one to be *morally correct*. When there is a conflict between someone either being morally correct or being politically correct, guess which *standard* wins if one desires continued commuting *iN tHE cAR?*

Regardless of the personal and professional damage done to the party or parties involved, the price of being *politically correct* **must**

iN tHE cAR

be made – **at all costs** – if one wishes to comfortably remain *iN tHE cAR*.

I refused to surrender my integrity in exchange for a casual ride *iN tHE cAR*. To me, the nonrefundable cost of that temporary ride (where the driver and most of the occupants lacked morals) was much too high of a price to pay. In that System, where integrity was frequently auctioned and sold to the *lowest bidder*, my personal and professional stance literally made me odd-man-out. Consequently, *I walked*.

The California Department of Corrections (CDC) has been affectionately dubbed, "The California Department of Corruption" and "The California Department of Censorship." While not totally dismissing those fluctuating titles, I would add my personal definition of CDC - "**C**hild **D**evelopment **C**enter" - as it pertains to the wannabe power brokers within that System.

These little spoiled children are in constant need of attention and pampering to help soothe their childish egos. It appears to be relatively easy, therefore, when their egos are bruised for these children's judgments - with their *miniature pea brains* and *frequent temper tantrums* - to become clouded.

Whether the issue deals with professional ethics or just simply professionalism, bruised egos oftentimes equate to clouded judgment and crisis management (the old knee-jerk form of managing). This management *style* ultimately leads to a less-than-satisfactory (and in fact, an undesirable) decision-making mechanism and outcome. By now, we've all probably heard of the old African proverb which states:

♦♦♦
"It takes a whole village to raise a child."
♦♦♦

As it pertains to this "**C**hild **D**evelopment **C**enter," Lonnie DeWitt states:

♦♦♦
"It takes all of CDC staff to help nurture its management; many, of whom, are not yet potty-trained!"
♦♦♦

Having had to help wipe my younger siblings' behinds and clean up baby poop, I certainly did not mind helping to potty-train these spoiled and obnoxious managers. What did bother me, however, was that these children had the audacity to haul around their own personal port-a-potty while whining to be pampered.

Over the years, I have learned that the major difference between the cub scouts and the California Department of Corrections, is that the cub scouts have *adult supervision and leadership.*

There can be no room for vindictiveness in a professional working environment. When one becomes too comfortable, complacency sets in - just as rigamortis sets in on a corpse. It is easy to juxtapose rigamortis with complacency, since *both* demand inactivity to be effective.

Across the State of California, within the CDC System, the suicide rate is high; the absenteeism rate is high; the levels of job dissatisfactors are high; and the gap of discontent and distrust between management and line employees continues to widen.

When one considers the multitude of negative stress factors that CDC manufactures, it is certainly conceivable that one day someone - who is already authorized to carry a weapon - will (God forbid) walk into a State building or a State institution and begin the mass murdering process in which we have all become so *routinely accustomed* during this past decade.

State officials will then realize that postal employees aren't the only *disgruntled* workers in a bureaucratic system who are capable of either selective or mass retaliation.

I charge the California Department of Corrections with promoting, condoning, exercising, and openly practicing institutional (racism), benign neglect and indifference toward its minority staff.

Since this **C**hild **D**evelopment **C**enter insists on treating minorities as its bastardized children then, I also charge CDC with performing multiple counts of incest!

State employees are asked to make personal sacrifices and pay high premiums into an account that is morally bankrupt. Racism (institutional or not), is a cancerous growth that self-feeds through ignorance, hatred, greed; and oftentimes insecurity.

California Department of Corrections, this is your wake-up call! I caution and challenge all of your supervisors and managers to revamp their personal, political and hidden agendas to exclude the present practices that perpetuate a hostile working environment which is continually fueled with fears and distrust. Those flames help contribute to CDC's corrupt System and to the obvious indifference that it continues to show toward inmates incarcerated in our State-wide penal institutions; to its parolees and to its minority staff.

Is it so difficult for one to expect (or even demand that) a State agency conforms to both practice and spirit of our laws governing equal treatment (and opportunities) for its citizens? I think not. But, why should they? After all, our managers within the California Department of Corrections are held accountable and responsible for both their actions and inactions *only* when such breach reaches the magnitude that would warrant the Director's personal involvement. Unfortunately, this must first demand his embarrassment through negative media attention. Hang on to your *stabilizer*, Mr. Director; you are obviously **stuck** in *hypocritical overdrive*. Brace yourself for a *very rough ride*.

No, all is not fine within the California Department of Corrections. It is facing and will continue to face unparalleled numbers of lawsuits involving staff and inmates. CDC managers are ill-equipped to effectively resolve issues (either on a personal or professional level) adversely affecting minority staff, parolees, inmates their families.

Much *lip service* (rhetoric) is given to the Department's **so-called** Peoples' Programs; however, as we all know, **"the road to hell is paved with good intentions!"** Chuck Knox once said:

> **"What you do speaks so clearly,**
> **I don't have to hear what you say."**

California Department of Corrections, your words have fallen on deaf ears while **your actions have left much to be desired.** Furthermore, I have *serious cause* to question your so-called, *"good intentions!"*
Talk to the hand, 'cause the ears aren't listening!

Now, let's shift gears for a moment. As a million-mile, accident-free (privately-owned vehicle) driver, I suppose that I am, somewhat, in a position to articulate my personal defensive driving philosophy. I developed an axiom that I dubbed *PLA* - *P*ositive *L*ane *A*dvantage. Ascribing to my *PLA* principle, I have been able to survive the *asphalt jungles* of interstate highways, freeways and the like.

Although I am *not* a *slow* driver (by any stretch of one's imagination), I am a defensive driver. As such, I consciously and deliberately choose the driving lane which offers both the optimum speed that I desire and an *effective escape* route in the event that it becomes necessary for me to either safely merge into another lane or totally exit the interstate/highway due to an emergency or hazardous situation. In essence, I drive to survive.

I consciously compare the art of driving with that of living since there is a direct correlation between the two. We drive defensively - we live defensively. Since, "the best defense is a good offense" prudent drivers must, therefore, contend with many arduous tasks of becoming both offensive and defensive drivers. In our daily lives, we must also live offensively to avoid sudden (and oftentimes costly) defensive maneuvers.

For the most part, I managed to avoid these man-made landslides, mudslides and boulders deliberately placed in my path as I traveled along *Life's Highways*.

Sadly, however, when one is traveling sixty-five miles an hour and a *mountain* (like the one that Montel Williams described in his book, *"Mountain, Get Out of My Way"*) suddenly appears - where nanoseconds earlier, there was none - a crash is inevitable.

Obviously, my crash (or, quite possibly, it was a *clash*) with the California Department of Corrections resulted in my premature (career) demise.

Fortunately, I am very safety conscious; therefore, I was wearing my seat belt. Now, guess what? I'm back and *still* **(steel) Black.** CDC must now **contend** (and **make amends**) with me!

It is apparent that the Department requires a complete face-lift; a total top-down scrub; a complete lobotomy and liposuction.

I would like to see an improved State correctional system, which may demand the immediate replacement of its current micro-managing nitwits whose over-zealousness and, *"good wood"* mentalities expound to the knee-jerk theory of conflict resolution.

Let's replace these folks with *real* managers who have clearly shown progressive and positive styles of leadership and who are sincerely concerned about the well being of their staff and the people that they are charged to supervise and protect.

In Vietnam, a popular slogan was:

> **"When I die, I'll go to heaven,**
> **'cause I've spent my time in hell!"**

The true impact of that slogan became more meaningful, to me, in my position as a parole agent. My *war* became one of personal and professional survival on *that* **Battlefield of Hell!**

The California Department of Corrections literally shoved me and my family into that *fiery pit* they call, *"fair and equitable."* It didn't seem to matter to Departmental managers that what they had done was unethical, immoral, illegal and clearly unjustified. The harder I struggled, the more they pushed. Our lives became a *living nightmare*.

Hundreds of thousands of my brothers and sisters in-arms have paid the supreme sacrifice for *US* to enjoy our freedoms. Yet, many of *US* are still restrained. **No, America, freedom is NOT really free!** The battlefield may have changed, but the *daily battle continues*.

It seemed as though I was feverishly spending my entire (bartered) Corrections career simply trying to *justify* my own existence while that System treated me like a penny-saver, mail order, back alley, garage sale, blue light special, community property prostitute.

Departmental officials have misguided priorities while cowardly seeking to add even more blind loyalists to its cadre of brainless warriors. Consider, for instance, the administrative *By-Law* discharges of several dozen (possibly, even, hundreds of) parolees annually. I am being very conservative and this is no joke.

Parole agents are required to submit annual reports for most parolees.

However, if the agent fails to submit this report in a timely manner, **the parolee is subsequently released from parole supervision - By Law - into the community.**

Although most parole agents' caseloads are (criminally) high, many agents do an outstanding job in avoiding these late submissions. However, I will give you a visual appreciation of this adverse impact. In San Jose alone, there was one parole agent who had thirteen parolees released into the community - *By-Law* - in one year!

This law is ludicrous and totally unacceptable. It presents very clear and definable safety concerns for all California residents and United States citizens and visitors. Yet, it is allowed to go unchallenged and unquestioned by CDC officials. Why?

This question should pose some serious political and social interest on this issue; especially, when one considers the *likely* potential for abuse.

I mentioned this issue to my supervisor who only reminded me that, "it was law." At that time, I told him, "If laws enacted it, laws can change it." I guess my comment warranted no response since that is exactly what I received. I often wondered how an issue of this gravity could be given so little attention. Is it possible that somehow CDC has taken advantage of this obvious **inappropriate law** for *self-gain*? Otherwise, why hasn't this law been challenged?

The possibilities of *unlimited abuse*, therefore, becomes *very real*; especially, when one considers that CDC officials now have the *legal means* to effect the premature release of a relative or friend from parole supervision - *By-Law* - into mainstream America.

I am confident that either a federal or congressional investigation into each of my allegations would uncover bags of **CDC filth** in that **family of dysfunctional degenerates.**

In the 1960's there was a *so-called* radical group known as The Weathermen. This group's premise was based on the following:

**"You don't have to have a weather vane
to see which way the wind is blowing!"**

By now, many of us ought to know, *"...which way the wind is blowing."*

The California Department of Corrections is on a non-stop collision course to *hell* unless its present philosophy (that encourages bigotry and sacrifices integrity) is reversed. Of course, that reversal must be accomplished with, *"all deliberate speed"* and *"by any [lawful] means necessary!"*

Speaking of, "reversal" please allow me to softly apply my brakes and place this vehicle into reverse before you begin to prematurely and harshly criticize me.

It's important (to me) that each of you gain a very personal and meaningful insight into the life of Lonnie Faustino DeWitt. To some of you, it may be of little significance that I was named after my Grandmother Gertie's second husband - a kind and sweet Filipino gentleman - Alberto Faustino Nadonsa.

But, that genealogical trivia obviously speaks very little of who *I am*. Therefore, just sit back, relax and allow me to chauffeur you as we begin to drive slowly forward and peek into the life of Lonnie Faustino DeWitt. Then, and only then, will you be able to fully appreciate my personal and professional irrepressible disgust while sharing my uncontrollable and caustic pain.

Chapter Two

The Valley

s a child growing up in the small, hot, dusty, agricultural town of El Centro, California, I was very content. After all, I lived with my mother, Alice; my father, James; two older brothers, James Edward and John; and a younger sister (although by only eleven months), Carol Ann.

I was told that I also had a younger brother, Donald Lester, who lived in a far away place called, "San Francisco" with my grandmother, Nellie (my mother's mom) and my grandfather, LC.

During my early childhood years, I really didn't remember Donald; but I was told that he once lived with us in El Centro until the doctors found out that he was allergic to the climate in *the Valley* - Imperial Valley - so, he was taken to live with our grandparents.

My other grandparents (Grandma Gertie and Grandpa James) and several cousins also lived in El Centro. My brother, James and Grandma Gertie were inseparable. James probably slept more nights over Grandma's house than he did at home. Mom did not seem to mind though, because we had a house full.

Growing up in a very small community during the 1940s and 1950s was truly a blessing. My siblings and I were taught the *basics* as they pertained to family values: respect, love, character, loyalty, honesty and integrity. Those virtues would later become the cornerstones of my character as I matured into adulthood.

El Centro was a community that literally looked out for each other. My brothers and I could ride our bikes for miles and people would always identify each of us as, "one of those DeWitt boys." My elementary school teacher, Mrs. Bassano, was also my dad's school teacher many years earlier.

After school, James and John would always either head for the fishing holes or look for pigeons to catch and later sell. They would repeatedly remind me that I was, "too young" to follow them. Sometimes, I did, at a distance, until one of their thrown rocks found its mark and I ran home crying.

Those hot, lazy, summer days of El Centro found us headed for *The Plunge*, our only public swimming pool. James and John didn't seem to mind me and Carol following them to the pool since many other kids our age also swam there. It was about a two-mile walk to *The Plunge* from our very small, two-bedroom home; however, both Carol and I knew better than to complain.

Because of our closeness in age, my sister and I would always find ourselves pairing off. We sort of *protected* each other.

Carol would always help me tie my shoelaces. Actually, she would tie them for me.

My sister and I would sit on the porch for hours, in the late evenings, counting the number of cars that went by in either direction. Each night we would *gamble* to see which one of us had the most cars driven in *our* direction. I must still owe Carol at least a million dollars!

Living in El Centro also taught me some of the hard realities of life. I quite vividly recall my entire family sitting on a curb after having been evicted from the projects. I don't recall any of the circumstances surrounding our eviction; however, that event has been permanently etched into my memory.

Mom and dad separated and later divorced. At the time, I felt that it wasn't a *big deal* since we had not seen our father in quite some time, anyway. When mom met Mr. Johnnie Ray Combs she was very happy; and so were we. They later married. Mr. Johnnie Ray (that's what we were told to call him) was a wonderful husband and father.

They were soon to add two new members to our large but loving family - Deborah Lynn and Johnnie Ray, Junior. Although I was only six years Deborah's senior, I carried her around on my bony hips everywhere I went. Deborah was my heart. Junior was born two years later.

My whole world seemed to end and yet begin at a very early age when God, in His infinite wisdom, beckoned my mother to come home. I was only ten.

I recall peering into a casket at a church and looked at someone who *resembled* my mother. But, that woman was much darker than my mom. I was later told that my mother (who had a light complexion) had lost so much blood that it actually made her complexion darker.

Although I really didn't relate that dark woman in the casket as being my mother, I somehow understood that my mother had died and that she would no longer be with me.

This personal tragedy was further aggravated by my grandmother (from San Francisco) who drove to El Centro and *snatched* James, John, Carol and me and took us to live with her, my grandfather and my younger brother, Donald (who I did not remember).

As we drove away from home in El Centro, I recall waving goodbye (with teary eyes) to Deborah and Junior, as they stood in the doorway - waving - not fully understanding the significance of what was really happening. But, then, how could they? Deborah was four and Junior was only two. In fact, neither Carol nor I fully understood.

Our family was devastated! We were physically and emotionally torn apart. Almost immediately following my mother's funeral services, we were driven to San Francisco where we were *forced* to live. None of us were allowed the common courtesy of going through the grieving process.

Consequently, each of us held onto the bitter memories of our mother's death and the cruel circumstances following her burial long after we became adults.

It wasn't until the Summer of 1992 (nearly thirty-five years later) that we all had the courage to hold a reunion at our mother's grave site. We finally released our emotions and laid aside some (not all) of the bitterness and hostilities that each of us had held onto for so long.

That reunion was the first time that all of my brothers and sisters (except Donald) gathered together in one place, at the same time, since our mother's death on September 26, 1957. We finally had closure.

My oldest brother, James, could no longer tolerate the mental and physical abuse to which our grandparents (mostly, our grandfather) subjected us. James boarded the Number 7 Haight-Ashbury Bus to 7th and Market Streets - the Greyhound Bus Station - where departed for El Centro. James was only thirteen years old when he *ran away* from home.

James and John showed much character. Although they had both secretly planned James' great escape, they still took time to complete their morning job of delivering the San Francisco Call Bulletin, the San Francisco Chronicle and the San Francisco Examiner newspapers.

John was next to leave. My grandfather beat John so often that John simply refused to cry. That, of course, angered our grandfather whose beatings escalated from the use of a belt to his using an extension cord to *discipline* us.

John then wrote James and complained about the cruel treatment that we were receiving. One Sunday morning, our father showed up, unannounced and unnoticed. All of us, except Carol (and Donald, of course), wanted to go live with our dad. Carol simply did not want to leave.

Although I desperately wanted to leave and get away from that abusive household, I was equally determined to stay and help look after my *baby* sister.

So, John left; and Carol and I stayed. James and John called that, **"good lookin' out"** on my behalf. To me, the words, **"good lookin' out"** represented the ultimate compliment or strokes that my older brothers could bestow upon me. It was a kind of triumphant acknowledgment that James and John *rarely* (and I do emphasize *rarely*) gave.

I have always been quite close to and very protective of Carol since our childhood. I recall buying her a coat when I received my very first paycheck from *Ma Brown's Restaurant* where I washed dishes after school. Even as an adult, I have flown halfway around the world to come to Carol's assistance. Again, **"good lookin' out."**

POLYTECHNIC

HIGH SCHOOL

Chapter Three
Class of `65

 knew that growing up in a big city, like San Francisco, wasn't going to be easy. But, I made it.

Like most Black families, of that era, our *roots* were deeply planted in a Baptist church. I regularly attended the El Bethel Baptist Church on Golden Gate Avenue, in San Francisco. I later joined and was baptized at El Bethel. I was very active in many church activities, including my membership in the Youth Choir and the Ushers' Board. I was also frequently called upon to speak as a youth speaker.

I attended Dudley Stone Elementary School, Marina Junior High School and I graduated from Polytechnic High School, where I was the Class (of 1965) Valedictorian. During my junior high and high school years, I was very active in sports and school politics, having held several class and general student body offices.

I really enjoyed my high school years. I worked two part-time jobs. In the mornings, I delivered newspapers; and in the evenings I washed dishes at Ma Brown's restaurant in the Marina District. During the summer months, I also worked part-time for a major department store while attending summer school. I attended summer school religiously - not because I needed the extra credits to graduate, but - because I needed an outlet to get away from home.

My grandfather and grandmother were very strict - to the point of cruelty. Even as a high school senior, I was not allowed to participate in most after school functions, including my own Senior Prom.

I recall starring (as George) in our high school play, *A Raisin in the Sun*. I had practiced many long hours for that play; and when the time came for my drama class to present the play to the public, my grandfather forbade me to participate because he disliked one of my lines, "Black brother, hell!"

I told my drama teacher to have a *fill-in* available, in the event that I failed to show for *curtain call*. Although my grandfather did not like it, I participated in the play anyway. My grandmother attended our opening night.

My grandfather would always beat us (except Donald) for trivial things with a *strap* (his belt). For whatever reasons, my grandfather offered us neither positive reinforcement nor encouragement. In fact, he rarely spoke, except when *disciplining* us.

Donald, on the other hand, received *VIP* treatment. He even ate different (and better) food than the rest of us. Needless to say, Donald was seldom disciplined; and when he was, it was mostly *verbal*. I really loved Donald. Privately, I also envied him, too. I secretly wished that my grandparents would give me the positive strokes that James and John infrequently gave me - the kind of strokes that Donald customarily received. James and John were, in essence, my heroes. I looked up to them - like a puppy wagging its tail - waiting for any signs of their approval.

During my senior year, I asked my grandparents to buy me a class ring. I really wanted a Polytechnic High School class ring. My grandparents told me that they did not have the money. So, I didn't get my ring. A few years later, when Donald graduated from high school, they paid cash for his brand new Ford Mustang.

Many years later, my wife, Ruthie, would buy me my Polytechnic High School class ring of 1965.

I recall that during my senior year, my grandfather whipped me so often that I was forced to confide with church members and with the late Mr. Harold Zimmerman, the Dean of Boys at *Poly*.

During the course of a *routine* whipping, I grabbed the belt and told my grandfather not to ever lay his hands on me again! I then left the house and turned myself into the juvenile authorities.

Because that system was unaccustomed to having a juvenile *turn himself in*, for *protection* against household abuse, I was treated like a criminal; handcuffed and placed in a *cell*. The following morning, juvenile staff could not figure out what to do with me. They wanted to send me to an in-house school; however, classes only went to the 8th or 9th grade. I had not committed a crime; therefore, they did not want me there. That day, several church members visited; and Mr. Zimmerman telephoned me and I told him what had happened. I spent another night in *juvy*.

The following day, my grandmother (who had been, *"embarrassed"* by this entire incident) showed up. She begged me to go home with her because, *"all of the church members were talking."* I did. My grandfather never hit me again. I did not hate my grandfather. In fact, I looked upon him with much pity. I knew that my grandfather *lacked something*; I just didn't know *what*.

Through it all, though, not once did I ever either verbally abuse or disrespect my grandfather. When he was on his deathbed, my grandfather asked that I - *not* Donald - come to his bedside and comfort him.

Even as a young adult, I was obedient and rushed to his side. Shortly thereafter, my grandfather slipped away. I cried.

My very best friend was Anthony Smith. We both attended Dudley Stone Elementary, Marina Junior High and Polytechnic High School together. Anthony and I both enjoyed sports and although he was much better than I, he would always make me *seem* competitive. I ran the 50- 100- and 220-yard dashes and the 440-yard relay as the anchorman.

Anthony also ran track and he was one of the better players on our *Poly* varsity football team. Another excellent football player was William (Gerald) Rice. Anthony and Gerald were good friends; however, Gerald and I couldn't say, "Let's get along!" He would always tease and make fun of me because my grandparents would not allow me to participate in many after school activities.

Anthony, on the other hand, seemed to either understand; or, at least tolerate my situation. Anthony was like a brother to me. One would probably describe Anthony as tall, dark and (unlike me) handsome. In retrospect, I probably looked like a shrimp standing next to him - kind of a Siskel and Ebert pair - a real *odd* combination. Nonetheless, Anthony was my *bud* and we *kicked it* together even after high school. The year we graduated (or, maybe, the following year), Anthony fathered a beautiful daughter named Phyllis Smith.

For the next several years, Anthony and I would always keep in contact with each other. Every time I took leave (vacation) from the military, I would always visit him and his mother in San Francisco. During one such visit, Anthony told me that one of his brothers had recently been murdered.

Anthony would, less than a year later, fall victim to the same fate. I had lost a very special friend. I lost a brother.

Anthony's mother, who for all those years I knew only as, "Ms. Smith," died a short time later; probably, from a broken heart.

To this day, I still have a photograph of Phyllis even though we have lost contact with each other.

Upon graduating from high school, I went job-hunting. The job market was plentiful, as I glanced through the *Help Wanted* advertisements in the *San Francisco Examiner* and *Chronicle*. Of all the job vacancies I answered, the one that I best remember required typing skills for a flexowriter-typist position.

During my interview, I took both a typing test and a written examination. I achieved a 94% score on the written examination; and my typing skills were equally impressive with an 85 word per minute errorless test result! To my amazement, however, I was not selected for the position even though the interviewer told me that I, *"fared considerably better"* than the other job applicants on both tests.

The interviewer appeared to be candid when he explained that although I was certainly qualified for that entry-level position, he felt that by the time I was thoroughly trained that I would, *"probably be drafted into the Army"* (since this was the height of the Vietnam Conflict).

The interviewer further explained that he would then be, *"forced"* to hire and train my replacement. In short, he suggested that I join the Army and, *"get it over with!"*

Well, I took his advice.... partially....I joined the United States Air Force.

Chapter Four

A Great Way of Life

hen I departed from my grandparents' home in San Francisco and as I boarded the Number 7 Haight-Ashbury bus, on the corner of Divisadero Boulevard and Haight Street, I felt tears trickling down my face because I knew at that moment that I had become a man and that I was now entering this big world alone. I knew that whatever challenges and problems I now faced that I would have to resolve them on my own. I glanced throughout the bus to see if anyone had noticed the tears in my eyes as I desperately tried to wipe my face.

I was on my way to becoming a man - an Airman. The bus slowly inched its way toward the Greyhound Bus Terminal where I would depart for the Oakland Military Induction Center.

My six weeks of basic military training at Lackland Air Force Base, Texas, were (or, so I thought at the time), pure drudgery; but, extremely rewarding. I really disliked being awakened in the middle of the night to either go marching, or to do physical exercises or, just to simply amuse the drill instructor.

Those six weeks also helped me tremendously in reinforcing the basis of my character, which now included *discipline*. From Lackland, I went to Amarillo Air Force Base, Texas, where I attended the Administration Specialist Technical School.

Since I had taken both Typing I and II in high school, I was far ahead the majority of students in my class. In fact, because of my excellent typing skills, I was required to take only one typing test.

My academic studies weren't as fortunate. I flunked my final test and had it not been for a somewhat empathetic instructor, I would not have been given a second chance to pass the examination - which I did....barely. I really wanted to pass that test because I had already received my first permanent assignment orders - to Oxnard Air Force Base, California - which would have certainly been canceled had I not successfully passed the examination. I felt proud and dumb at the same time.

At Oxnard, I met and established lifelong friendships with many people, which includes my first Air Force supervisor, Leonard Marsh.

One of the more memorable events, to me, was when I first saw the (then) top secret U-2 surveillance (spy) aircraft take-off. What a beautiful sight!

I truly loved my native State of California; and I really enjoyed my assignment at Oxnard. Still, I felt empty, restless, and curious about the world around me. Surely, I didn't join the Air Force to simply stay in California.

I wanted to see more of the United States and the world. The sheer thought of traveling to a foreign country that was ravished by war excited me (which was to be expected of a wet nose nineteen year-

iN tHE cAR

old). Yet, those same thoughts also frightened me.

Nonetheless, I volunteered to be reassigned to the Republic of South Vietnam. Like so many others who preceded me, my volunteer statement was expeditiously processed.

I spent one year and two days at DaNang Air Base (1966 - 1967), where I personally witnessed and heard tales of heroism, death, and atrocities committed by *all* countries involved. I was medically evacuated (airlifted) to CamRahn Bay Hospital - a hospital in South Vietnam - where I remained thirty days after contracting an acute case of hepatitis.

While in the hospital, the facility where I worked (at DaNang) was blown up during a nightly attack by the Viet Cong. My comments were, **"God lookin` out!"**

My tour of duty in South Vietnam was extremely challenging and professionally rewarding. At the end of my tour, I was awarded my first, of many, Air Force Commendation Medals.

The bonds of friendship and respect that were shared between my fellow airmen and me formed an unbreakable commitment of trust, love and loyalty.

Most Vietnam veterans (who are willing to talk about it) will admit that DaNang Air Base was frequently under attack by the Viet Cong. We received what seemed like nightly attacks of small arms, rockets, mortars and other destructive weaponry.

One of the more memorable attacks found us, as usual, scurrying to our sand bunkers (which were just outside our barracks). Upon taking a head count, I realized that one man was unaccounted for and possibly still inside the building. Without hesitation, I immediately rushed back into the barracks and found my friend (who reeked of alcohol); threw him across my shoulder and ran back outside into the safety of the bunker.

In retrospect, I am certain that my friend would openly characterize my actions as, *"good lookin` out."*

I felt so fortunate in having been able to represent and assist our Nation during those times of high public resentment and national controversies. Although I was not on the front lines fighting (very few

Air Force personnel were) my job in providing mail services to our entire American Forces, Allied Forces and civilian contractors, was rewarding.

We all took pride in knowing that on Christmas Day, 1966, not one piece of mail remained undelivered at the DaNang Aerial Mail Terminal.

At any overseas location - especially, in a war zone - mail is oftentimes the only link between military personnel and their loved ones. We realized the importance of our job and the impact that it had on troop morale. Therefore, we were all determined to provide the best possible mail services; even under the most hostile environment.

To me, the **United States Air Force** was - and remains - **a great way of life!**

I fully supported (mentally and physically) our role in Vietnam. Still, I felt sad for the hundreds of thousands of lives lost by all countries. I tried to imagine how some Vietnamese must have felt about *US* being in their country. For that reason, while the war was going on all around me, I wrote this poem:

◆ ◆ ◆

Vietnam: Mirrored Visions

.... and when we glanced back at our, "mission" -
a bloody, lifeless, battlefield of shattered lives
and short-lived dreams - we took solace in
knowing that our involvement was *only* a
conflict....

We sit, waiting, trembling and frightened...
    huddled together in a crowded room.
The dreadful sounds we fear,
    may soon be coming near.
This scene is repeated,
    many times fold.....

and each time we gather,
> the bombs take their toll.

Last week it was Nguyen,
> the week before, Nam Dee.

Yesterday, it was Dinh,
> who knows, tonight it might be me!

We hope and pray
> the bombs never come;

but, we know dammed well,
> the Yankee'll bring his guns.

He comes with, "Democracy and Freedom"
> for all mankind.

Well, it must be on the tip of a warhead,
> `cause, I've seen my people buried in pine!

Our Country is divided;
> and our Government has never been.

We hope some day to get it together;
> but, it must be within.

My people are weary of this war…
> tired of being divided.

You say, "There'll always be a North and South."
> Bullshit! We are ALL of the same House.

The bombs drop;
> napalms flare.

The Yankees are on their way home now,
> leaving death and destruction in the air.

A motherless child
> stands alone in grief.

No comforting words are spoken;
> she hears only the fading sounds of feet.

A newlywed widow
> cries in despair.

Had it not been for *US*,
> she wouldn't be crying there.

A fatherless son,

    whose heart burns with hate,
vows to the heavenly gods,
    he'll revenge *US* someday.
France was first;
    but, to no avail.
The United States, second…
    we'll send 'em to hell!
A distant, familiar sound coming near;
    my mind snaps back into reality!
We are still tense and frightened.
    I wonder endlessly, are the bombs coming for me?
Now, they are overhead…
    their whistling load comes near!
Women scream; men cry;
    premonitions fill their eyes!
Suddenly, a tremendous roar!
    Windows shatter, metal flung…
Is this my doom?
    I am only twenty-one!
A deafening sound;
    intense pain!
I bid a silent farewell to life,
    as I enter death's domain.
They sit, waiting, trembling…

◆ ◆ ◆

Whether or not you agree (with the feelings, perceptions and fears that I experienced in 1967, as a 20-year old), is unimportant to me at this point of my life. What mattered most, to me, was that during my tour in Vietnam, I began to question my own mortality as I witnessed the lives of so many young people - my age - being prematurely forfeited. I even began to question and seek answers to the *real* reasons why American and Allied Forces were supporting that war effort. Although I found more questions than answers, I continued to serve my Country, with distinction.

When our Freedom Bird (Pan American Airways) taxied down Saigon's war-torn runway, feelings of joy, relief, excitement, and anticipation of joyful reunions filled the air. Some of us even whispered a silent prayer as we shed tears for our fallen comrades who would not be returning home.

After having served one year in hell, we (those of us who were *fortunate* to survive) were finally returning to the United States of America. We were going home.

Our plane was scheduled to arrive at San Francisco International Airport. After circling that airport because of heavy fog, our flight was eventually diverted to Oakland Airport. As we left the aircraft, many of us (including me) kissed the ground. The horrors of war, coupled with our having to circle above San Francisco's Airport (for what seemed like an eternity), necessitated that act of thankfulness.

Although we all knew not to expect marching bands and a ticker-tape parade, few of us fully realized the apathetic feeling that had penetrated our Nation while we were in Vietnam serving, fighting and dying.

Unfortunately, for most of us, we returned to an *UN*-United States. We returned to a place that we had never known; a place that we could not understand. It seemed that we had either distanced ourselves from the rest of the Nation; or, the Nation had distanced itself from us - its military men and women - who faithfully served and sacrificed in the uniform of our Country.

It seemed that because we unselfishly fulfilled our patriotic duties and served our Country that we were ostracized and labeled, "baby killers" while those who evaded the draft were given a hero's welcome.

I am reminded of an (unpublished) article that I wrote reflecting my views about our involvement in the Persian Gulf:

❖ ❖ ❖

Objective Citizenry

Having spent one tour of duty in the war-torn Country of South

Vietnam, I wish to share my thoughts - both as a disciplined military veteran and as a private citizen - about the merits of objectivity in citizenship.

Consistent with the parameters of the United Nations Security Council Resolution 678 and, after fully exploring and exhausting all avenues and alternatives available to him, only then did President Bush, with the approval of Congress, give the green light for Operation Desert Storm. In the midst of our involvement in the Persian Gulf War, the world will, once again, take America's pulse.

The conscious of America will be judged and our unity, perseverance, and discipline as a united people will be heavily tasked. Let's seize this opportunity - however unfortunate - to show the world that the United States of America is, and will continue to be, a United States.

Let's fully support our President and show him that he was right on target in his (disregarded) letter to Iraqi President, Saddam Hussein:

♦♦♦

> *"...You may be tempted to find solace in the diversity of opinion that is American democracy. You should resist any temptation. Diversity ought not be confused with division. Nor should you underestimate, as others have before you, **America's will...**"*

♦♦♦

The late Dr. Martin Luther King, Jr., once said, *"The greatness of America is the right to protest for right."*

We must neither give up that right nor abuse the right to protest. I sadly acknowledge that we have some protesters who have exceeded the *boundaries of protest* and penetrated the realms occupied by impulsive radicals.

Let's rally to the occasion. Let's lay aside our political differences; let's lay aside our cultural and sub-cultural differences; let's lay aside our petty bickering of race and color and start *thinking* **Red**, **White** and **Blue**! Let's put an end to this hair-splitting of social issues by verbally (with tongue-in-cheek) supporting our troops overseas; yet, protesting our involvement in the war! Let's stop this fence straddling and cash in our airline tickets – we've obviously missed our plane.

In our comparatively short history as a Nation, America has learned that **freedom really isn't free**. Our American troops in combat are committed to pay the supreme sacrifice in order that our future generations may enjoy the freedoms that we have become so routinely accustomed.

As private citizens we, too, may someday (God forbid) be called upon to mobilize our forces to defend our Great Land. Do we stand vigilant and ready, America? The cliché, "United we stand, divided we fall," may be trite; but, it's true and appropriate.

I refuse to debate the merits of this war. I will neither second-guess our Congress nor our President's decision to liberate Kuwait. The votes were counted; the decision was made; and our troops are now fighting a war. There's no further room to debate and protest.

Let's fully support our President and our troops in the Persian Gulf and unanimously hope that they kick ass and come home to a sensitive and caring Nation.

President Bush's distinguished military record speaks for itself. His bravery, while under hostile fire, is certainly consistent with his actions now as President of the United States of America.

Yes, Mr. President (Commander-in-Chief), we know that this will be a long and costly war; yet, we believe that history will undoubtedly prove that the United Nations and more specifically, the United States, will emerge victoriously. Yes, Mr. President, even when the count of body bags rise, we will still affirm our loyalty to you and to our Great Nation.

In closing, I would be remiss not to include a passage by Mr. John Stuart Mill, a 19th Century philosopher:

♦ ♦ ♦

"War is an ugly thing, but not the ugliest of things: the decayed and degraded state of moral and patriotic feeling which thinks nothing worth a war, is worse."

♦ ♦ ♦

As a Nation, we can ill-afford that, *"decayed and degraded* (Vietnam-era complex) *state of moral and patriotic feeling,"* of which Mr. Mill spoke. I pray that God, in His infinite wisdom, will forever pour His cup of endless blessings over these, United States of America.

♦ ♦ ♦

The Vietnam Conflict tore into the heart of America as no other war in its history; including the Civil War, where brother fought against brother.

To this day, America still suffers from the deep wounds that penetrated its very soul. These wounds that seem to linger and manifest themselves through decades of public distrust and resentment toward our government and its leaders.

As a positive side note, during the 1994 Christmas season, I shared my Vietnam experience with our Nation's Military Forces Commander-in-Chief - The President of the United States of America - The Honorable William Jefferson Clinton. In November 1994, I sent President Clinton a copy of my poem, *Vietnam - Mirrored Visions*.

The President's genuinely warm and *extremely rapid response* is included in its entirety on the following page:

THE WHITE HOUSE
WASHINGTON

January 11, 1995

Dear Lonnie:

I appreciate your taking the time to write, and I want to thank you for the material you enclosed.

It's important to me that I hear the thoughts and experiences of people who care about the future of America and the world. Our nation faces many challenges as we prepare for the next century. I am seeking the most innovative approaches to address those challenges. Thank you for sharing your ideas with me.

Sincerely,

Bill Clinton

Chapter Five

Men, Women and Colored

 y next assignment was to Norton Air Force Base, California, where I would stay only nine months before volunteering for and being accepted to a special duty assignment with the Headquarters, Office of Aerospace Research (HQ OAR) and the Headquarters, Office of Scientific Research (HQ OSR). Both organizations were co-located in several offices of a fourteen-story high rise complex in downtown Arlington, Virginia.

By now, I had proposed marriage to my childhood sweetheart, the former Ruthie Louise Thorn of Shreveport, Louisiana. In June of 1968, we had planned to have a dual wedding with Ronald and Doris who were and still are lifelong friends of ours. However, my military orders created a slight problem since I had to be in Virginia by May of that year.

My fiancée and I decided to wed on April 13, 1968. We asked our pastor at El Bethel Baptist Church, the late Dr. D.D. Manning Jackson, to perform the ceremony. Our quaint wedding ceremony was performed in the Pastor's Study (a small office of the church).

My duty in Arlington was certainly different. Military personnel were authorized to wear civilian clothing as we interacted daily with top civilian officials.

Ruthie, our son, Kenslo (Ken), and I enjoyed the scenic tours of our Nation's Capital, Washington DC. The cost of living in that area, however, was extremely high. In fact, I had to work a second full-time job to financially survive. I actually worked a 96-hour week for eight consecutive months.

The Headquarters was scheduled to deactivate; therefore, I requested and received an assignment to Japan. This change of assignment would allow me, my wife and now two boys, Ken and Lonnie, Jr., to visit our many relatives and friends in California prior to departing for our overseas assignment.

The drive from Arlington, Virginia to San Francisco, California (by way of Shreveport, Louisiana) was unforgettable! It was the summer of 1970 when I first (to my knowledge) experienced and suffered the humiliation of overt racism.

My family and I drove to a public service station in Mississippi and asked for service. Although *satisfactory* service was given, when I asked to use the men's room, I was directed to the corner of the station where I noticed three restrooms clearly marked **Men, Women and Colored**. I simply could not believe that this type of overt racial discrimination *still* existed in the 1970s. Little did I realize that I would, once again, feel the sting of **American Racism** two decades later.

I used the *Men* restroom; however, nothing was said. The suffocating stench emanating from that restroom made it almost unbearable to use; and clearly uncomfortable to *rest*. I later wondered if the *Colored* restroom was incredibly filthy as the *Men* restroom.

After driving several more miles, my car radiator began to overheat. It was then that I learned that the service station attendants had poured dirt into my radiator.

While traveling through Mississippi, my family and I were actually refused entrance into several public restaurants. The outwardly displayed signs that read:

"We reserve the right to refuse service to anyone"

were taken literally by the locals.

I experienced extreme difficulty in trying to comprehend how those narrow-minded people could *allow* us (Blacks) into their kitchens to cook and eat; yet, they would not permit us in their dining facilities to be served over-the-counter! I simply could not understand the abnormal mentality of anyone who would allow a traveler into a kitchen (where food was prepared) rather than to serve that person over-the-counter.

I was determined not to belittle my family and myself by eating food in somebody's *back kitchen*. I attempted to drive through the entire State of Mississippi without eating. I lost.

My own hunger pains and the continued discomfort of my family forced me to stop the car and place my carry-out order of cheeseburgers and french fries in somebody's *back kitchen*.

We had driven about two miles before we realized that our cheeseburgers were *accidentally wrapped* - minus the cheese and the burgers.

Although I did give *brief* thought to going back and reporting the *discrepancy*, my wife and I decided that we would simply eat the french fries and the burger buns and continue our trip.

Conversely, I happily and vividly recall the time when my family and I experienced vehicle difficulty while traveling through Alabama. A White family came to our rescue! They treated us with much dignity, kindness and respect.

Although I did not ask for their assistance, they *insisted* on helping us. Each of them was truly a Godsend. Thank God that we *still* have some good people (of every color) in America.

The flight from Travis Air Force Base, California to Yokota Air Base, Japan was very smooth and enjoyable.

We traveled throughout Japan and met many wonderful Japanese who were anxious to assist us when we became lost (which was a routine occurrence). Many of the Japanese were eager to speak and proudly demonstrate their knowledge of the English language to us. Our four-year assignment in Japan was nothing less than outstanding.

My first Air Force mentor, Chief Master Sergeant (Hank) Motomatsu, was one of the most brilliant and exceptional Administrators in the Far East. *The Chief* taught me a very important element of administration: *documentation*. He would always say, "Sergeant DeWitt, if it's not documented, it didn't happen!"

As each of you continue reading *iN tHE cAR* you will gain a greater understanding and appreciation of *the Chief's* wisdom and the importance that he placed on *documentation*. Hopefully, you will agree that I learned my lessons well.

My youngest son still talks of returning to Japan (his first home). In fact, my wife continues to speak of our tour in Japan with much fondness.

My assignment to Travis Air Force Base, California from Japan was virtually uneventful. While assigned to the Western District Headquarters of the United States Air Force Postal and Courier Service (USAFPCS), I traveled to the eight Western States and performed staff visits to twenty-six Postal Service Centers. The experience and professional exposure that I gained through my travels were personally and professionally gratifying and tremendously rewarding.

When USAFPCS was scheduled for deactivation, I went job-hunting. The First Sergeant of the 60th Air Base Group, Chief Master

Sergeant Bobby A. Kelley, interviewed me for the Chief of Unit Administration position - working directly for him. He was more than pleased with my credentials and asked me if I would, "work with" him. I did.

The rapport and respect that Chief Kelley and I established were remarkable. He was a truly gifted and honorable man. I closely observed Chief Kelley as he daily interacted with all enlisted personnel. He was a master in communication skills and I wanted so badly to emulate him. The Chief was highly respected throughout Travis Air Force Base and the surrounding communities of Fairfield, Suisun and Vacaville.

When Chief Kelley received his permanent change of station orders to March Air Force Base, California, I immediately began looking for another job. I knew that whoever took his place simply could not measure up to Chief Kelley's professionalism and high ethical standards.

My premature job-hunting was short-lived.

Chapter Six

Ambassador in Blue

It was one of the proudest moments in my military career. All of my hard work and dedication were finally being recognized. A representative of the prestigious Military Airlift Command (MAC) Inspector General (IG) Team had actually asked me if I would consider volunteering for the Team. Even if it meant leaving my native State of California - to be stationed at Scott Air Force Base, Illinois - I just knew that my answer would be affirmative.

By the way, just where is Illinois? I quickly made some telephone calls to a few military friends that I knew had been stationed there. They gave me a pretty good idea of where the base was located, "...near Belleville, New Baden and Mascoutah, Illinois; just east of East St. Louis."

It really came as no surprise to me when my office staff anxiously and excitedly informed me that a Captain Joubert (pronounced, "Jo Bear") from the MAC/IG called for me and asked that I return his call. I pretended not to share in their excitement; but my pulsating heartbeat and, by now, my moistened hands probably gave me away.

As I dialed the unfamiliar number, I sensed a bit of history about to take place. Little did I realize that my telephone call would change the course of my entire military career. The voice on the other end of the telephone was neither warm nor cold. It was the voice of an impatient, hurried military man. One, who had, or at least wanted to give the impression as such, little time for formalities. "Hello, Captain Joubert? This is Sergeant DeWitt; I'm returning your call."

My telephone call had ended almost as abruptly as it began. I had been accepted to be a part of a major command inspector general team. This simply had to be the epitome of my military career (or so it seemed at the time).

Shortly afterwards, I began preparing for my departure from Travis to Scott Air Force Base, Illinois by way of Norton Air Force Base, California, where I would receive five days of classroom training on inspection techniques.

This short-notice reassignment gave me less than ninety days to, "be in place." As do most military personnel, I learned to accept and handle personal sacrifices. One, of which, was to temporarily leave my family and make necessary arrangements for them to join me at a later date.

By now, Ruthie and I had been thoroughly acclimated to the military and its short-notice deployment requirements. Nonetheless, ours was a sad and heartfelt farewell.

The drive through Southern California to Norton Air Force Base was uneventful. My entire week of intensified inspector general training, on the other hand, was exciting and thoroughly informative. I found the instructors to be highly qualified in their respective (specialty) fields and the subject areas were well tailored and course-specific.

Graduation Day found me on the highway again; but, this journey would take me out of California and across several other States until I reached......what was that place again? Oh yeah, Illinois. I drove through the main gate of Scott Air Force Base at exactly 0730 hours (7:30 AM), on the last day of August 1977.

This prestigious, two-year assignment would prove to be the catalyst for my professional growth and high visibility. As an Administrative Inspector, I traveled throughout the continental United States and to several foreign countries. It was rewarding for me to be in the position to not simply identify discrepant administrative areas but, to assist my fellow administrators and help them back on the *road to recovery*. I also took much pride in acknowledging areas of excellence and individual professionalism.

During the course of my inspection efforts, numerous base personnel would frequently compliment me on my conduct of inspection and my professional appearance and demeanor. Needless to say, inspectors are also inspected. I became acutely accustomed to virtually living in a *fishbowl*.

As a senior noncommissioned officer, I was often asked to either give presentations or speak to audiences on a myriad of subjects. To that end, I also wrote and published several articles in which two are included below:

Sensitivity: A Key to Effective Supervision

Let there be no question about it...there is no quick and easy, step-by-step solution to effective supervision. There is no such thing as a born supervisor, or an instant course in successful supervision. There are, however, hundreds of books on this subject; and each has its own merits.

As a blue-suiter, I have found that a leader who is sensitive to the needs of his subordinates is usually an effective supervisor who obtains the utmost in performance from his coworkers. But, wait a minute! Just what does it mean to be **sensitive***?*

The American Heritage Dictionary defines **sensitive** *as "Responsive to the external conditions or stimulation; susceptible to the feelings of others." The latter phrase reflects my personal sentiments on this subject.*

Let's keep everything in proper military perspective - mission first. Now, let's be realistic. Without our greatest asset - people, there would be no mission! The number of stripes on one's sleeves does not measure his intelligence or superiority over another. It merely represents a person's status within the military establishment.

As such, a senior individual should not "talk down" to a person of lesser rank. Treat everyone on the same scale, and bear in mind a quote from General Pershing:

"In the social order in which one person is officially subordinated to another, the superior, if he is a gentleman, never thinks of it, and the subordinate, if he is a gentleman, never forgets it."

An effective supervisor is always on the alert for radical changes in a subordinate's attitude, duty performance and even obvious physical and mental deviations. Although the Air Force provides a multitude of highly qualified professional technicians and counselors, the responsibility is often on the immediate supervisor to detect and channel these individuals to the proper source.

Simply stated, supervisors must be responsive and keenly interested in the welfare of their subordinates, on- and off-duty. Get my drift?

As the Pendulum Swings

Like people, attitudes, concepts and policies often change with every tick of the clock. Hopefully, these changes have been beneficial to our men and women in uniform, without surrendering our commitments for world peace nor compromising the preservation of our great country.

The constant momentum of the pendulum found the image of the armed forces changed drastically since the old Beetle Bailey/pot bellied sarge era. No longer are airmen and noncommissioned officers assigned menial and routine daily tasks often associated with uneducated and illiterate workers. Now, having realigned the pendulum properly on its axis, the "noncom" is placed in a position of leadership and authority; and his expertise and knowledge are often sought. Today's NCO is a welcome inclusion in the decision-making process at all levels of command.

All too often, subordinates view their supervisor as "the establishment," "management," or "the man upstairs" rather than a human being whose knowledge and continued demonstrated performance have resulted in his progression through the ranks into his present leadership and managerial role. Yes, it's difficult to believe that the "Ole Chief" was once a one-striper himself who was taken under his supervisor's wings and nurtured to his present "noncom" status. Today's noncommissioned officer demands loyalty, honesty, integrity, dedication, consideration, compliance, and a total commitment by his subordinates and of himself.

Sounds like a lot of heavy demands, huh? You betcha! Hitch a ride on the pendulum and you'll find that the demands get greater while the rewards become more abundant.

Management by objective has become an effective management tool used by supervisors at all levels, wherein each worker feels a part of his personal contributions to management. This advanced manage-

ment technique, which was adopted from a highly successful civilian industry, is now taught in all Air Force management courses of instruction for officers, NCOs and airmen. The pendulum moves on.

Our female force, which comprises seven percent of the total Air Force strength, has become an integral part and major asset to the Air Force. No longer are females, by virtue of their sex, relegated duties of serving coffee and performing general office work.

Instead, they occupy every level of management and directly contribute to its smooth and efficient operation. Discrimination, in any form, within the armed forces, is becoming a thing of the past.

Yes, the armed forces have traveled a great distance; and the Air Force, being its youngest member, has added enormous dimensions to the defense of our great land and to the free world. The pendulum beckons every blue-suiter to personally contribute toward its upward trend in mission accomplishment. If we, within the USAF, want to continue spiraling ahead, then we owe it to ourselves, our superiors and our country to give the best we've got to give. And while speculating future achievements, one may reasonably deduce greater advancements and better changes within the Air Force, "as the pendulum swings."

God blessed us with our lovely daughter, Shaneé Faustina, (*my Father's Day gift*) in 1983. Shaneé was born in Victorville, California, just prior to our four-year assignment to Camp O'Donnell Air Station (Capas Tarlac), Republic of the Philippines.

Although unknowingly (and certainly unworthy), I became part of an historical legacy when I assumed my First Sergeant duties (with Lt. Col. Paul H. Miller, Commander) at that air station. I learned that in 1942, 70,000 American and Filipinos (who defended the Bataan Peninsula), were captured by the Japanese and forced to march their final eight miles from Capas to Camp O'Donnell during the infamous Bataan Death March. Only 54,000 reached the Camp.

No, America, freedom is *NOT* really free!

I loved my military family and it was a difficult decision but I decided to *hang up my uniform* while stationed at Chanute Air Force Base, Illinois. As a Senior Master Sergeant, it seemed as though I had more stripes than a baby zebra.

The Base Commander, Colonel Dennis Murphy, and his lovely wife, Kathleen, gave my family and me a very warm and heartfelt retirement luncheon where many enlisted personnel and their families attended to wish us the very best that life had to offer.

From my humble enlistment in 1965, as a basic trainee, until my honorable retirement as a First Sergeant in 1988, I represented the United States of America (both domestic and abroad) as its *Ambassador in Blue*.

My distinguished and honorable years of servitude to my Country were, without exception, fond and memorable years.

Chapter Seven

An Arrogant, Smart-ass, You-Know-What

After having served twenty-three years, two months, and eleven days in the United States Air Force, I felt that I was totally prepared, both mentally and physically, to face Corporate America.

I was intimately familiar with the daily discipline and rigorously precise war games played by American military and Allied Forces. To this day, I still cherish my 13th Air Force medallion that reflects my active participation at Kim Hae Air Base, Republic of South Korea, during Team Spirit 1986 (a joint military exercise).

For the most part, Air Force leaders demanded that the application of standards be maintained, enforced and uniformly applied to personnel at all echelons of command.

Little did I know, however, that my awesome responsibilities as an Air Force First Sergeant would not adequately prepare me for the *games* played by staff employed within the California Department of Corrections where there were no *uniformed application of standards*. The *Director's Rules* simply applied to some members; not all.

I had mistakenly believed that my Bachelor of Science Degree in Business Management and three Associate Degrees would provide the necessary catalyst toward my upward mobility, in my newly chosen career, with the California Department of Corrections. I also believed that my credentials would earmark me as an articulate professional having a solid educational background with demonstrated career goals and objectives.

I felt that by my *playing by the rules* would somehow *exempt* me from being subjected to discriminatory practices.

Unfortunately, however, as the pages in my life began to unfold, I became increasingly aware that my academia achievements along with my hundreds of hours of managerial training, worldwide travels, and lifelong experiences, would eventually become negative factors and cause grave concern among other California Department of Corrections supervisors and managers. They would soon view me simply as an arrogant, smart-ass, you-know-what.

I simply had no clue that CDC management held the word *equal* with *contempt*. Amendment XIV to the United States Constitution states that:

"All persons born or naturalized in the United States, and subject to the jurisdiction thereof, are citizens of the United

States and of the State where they reside. No State shall....deny any person within its jurisdiction the *equal protection of the laws.*"

I soon learned that CDC managers played the *Rule* or *Ruin* game; and they played for *keeps*.

To further emphasize my point, the Declaration of Independence states:

"…**We hold these truths to be self-evident that all men are created *equal*, that they are endowed by their Creator with certain unalienable Rights, that among these are Life, Liberty and the pursuit of Happiness….**".

While we may be, "endowed by our Creator" with certain *equal rights*, the California Department of Corrections has blatantly shown that *some people* are **more equal** than *others*.

I certainly cannot speak for anyone else; but I find it extremely difficult to work for someone who is, by all standards, *stupid*. Of course, I am using the word *stupid* loosely, because I merely meant that the boss appeared not to have both oars in the water.

You know the kind of boss who doesn't play with a *full deck*. Yes, the same man (or woman) who, when the good Lord said, "brains" and the boss thought He said, "train" and asked for a, "slow" one.

Oftentimes, these poor excuses for managers and supervisors were simply promoted to their, "highest level of incompetence" (the Peter Principle) because of either nepotism or CDC's *upward mobility triangle*:

"who you know - who you owe - who you blow"

I recall working for a Correctional Sergeant, at Folsom Prison, who could not spell. However, rather than ask a Correctional Officer, this Sergeant found it less intimidating to ask a convict to help him (the Sergeant) write a report. How absurd! Nonetheless, that's the kind of mentality that our managers and supervisors in CDC consistently demonstrate.

Labels. It's truly unfortunate that each of us is *labeled* (rightly or wrongly) by these wannabe (self-described) power brokers. Sadly, more often than not, a *negative* label is attached to a Black person while a White person (who exhibits similar qualities) is given a *positive* label.

For instance, a Black man who is responsive and shows creativity is labeled as *arrogant* while his White counterpart is labeled as, *"A real go-getter; head and shoulders above the rest."*

Therefore, when anyone is *perceived* as (and subsequently labeled) a *liability* (*a threat*) rather than an *asset*, then his or her tenure within that organizational structure becomes, at best, restrictive and limited.

You say, "Invest in America." Even E.F. Hutton will advise potential investors when to cut their losses in the event there is a *negative return* on *any* investment. While I clearly recognize that America does **not** *owe* me anything; still, I do believe that, as a citizen, I am entitled to *equal rights and protection under the law.*

It seems as though CDC officials have given me a negative return on my five-year investment; therefore, while cutting my losses I also intend to expose and validate *some* of the ills and perils that Black (and other minority) correctional peace officers face, while employed, in that corrupt and insensitive System.

That *boy* label that seems to eternalize itself within the Black community from *cradle-to-grave* has got to cease. How many years of servitude must I give my Country before my label changes from *boy* to *man*; and I am considered an *equal* in that I have *paid my dues* to America? At age fifty-one, I would like to believe that I am no longer a *boy*; or, maybe that simply makes me a *grown boy* with an *arrogant* attitude.

To me, most CDC officials suffer from *brain farts* that seriously inhibit rational thinking and lend itself to irrational behavior.

I have, over the years, developed an extremely low tolerance for professional ignorance.

While we no longer label our restrooms - *men, women* and *colored* - the labels and markings are still evident and clearly visible in the workforce. Labels that forbid friendships are all too evident. For instance, let two or three minorities gather together during lunch or simply by happenstance in an office environment and then, closely observe the facial expressions and reactions of the White workforce as it feels an imminent threat of a perceived conspiracy.

Corporate Corrections has deliberately placed restrictions on its minority workforce (which include females) to minimize their opportunities while restricting any possibility for *unlimited* upward mobility and career progression. These and other critical issues are routinely ignored by Corrections officials as they systematically pay millions of dollars of California taxpayers' hard earned money each year to satisfy administrative and court-ordered financial **stipulations** and **settlements**.

That ominous *glass ceiling* is, therefore, nothing more than a corporate glass casket that has physically, emotionally, and financially enshrined and stagnated its professional minority workforce.

Yes, the California Department of Corrections has much bigger problems and greater challenges that it must quickly resolve. While some White correctional officers are busily etching racist symbols onto the butts of State-issued weapons, high profile and dangerous inmates are *allowed* to frequently escape into the community.

Even the Department's *routine* settling of million dollar lawsuits (that are directly proportionate to the numbers of ignorant managers it employs), demands an immediate audit investigation.

A group called *S.P.O.N.G.E.*, an acronym for the "**S**ociety for the **P**revention **O**f **N**iggers **G**etting **E**verything, is comprised of some White correctional officers at the California Institute for Men in Chino. The overt activities of *S.P.O.N.G.E.* are simply typical examples of how CDC managers have consistently and repeatedly opted to look the other way while White racism rears its ugly head.

Come on, **C**hildren, *recess* is over. Let's all get out of the ***sand box*** and take our little naps.

That **C**hild **D**evelopment **C**enter – like all children – along with *S.P.O.N.G.E.*, needs to be ***S.O.A.K.E.D.*** (***S***panked ***O***ccasionally ***A***nd ***K***issed ***E***very ***D***ay). That's *real* **tough love!**

Chapter Eight

R-e-s-p-e-c-t

J stood staring down the dimly lit halls of Old Folsom Prison. The chatter and noise that echoed loudly across the granite walls bespoke of the *family* residing therein. A *family* of thieves, murderers, child-molesters, and a few *innocent* people who, by their personal accounts, were merely victims of our criminal justice system.

I cannot, in good conscious, totally dismiss and ignore the cries of, "innocent" from a few *convicted* felons. The overwhelming evidence of ethics violations that we have seen during this past decade has taught

US that our criminal justice system has some very serious judicial flaws.

Some of our judges, district attorneys and lawyers are occasionally arrested and convicted for criminal offenses that range from bribery, suppressing crucial testimony (in a court of law) to possession of child pornography. The sad reality is that we rely on these *sick* individuals to **treat *US* fairly.**

Nonetheless, my job was to supervise these convicted felons and not take either a legal or personal position regarding either their guilt or innocence. I was a professional correctional officer.

When I arrived at Folsom State Prison as a newly assigned correctional officer, I immediately began the process of playing the *PIE* - *P*ermanent *I*ntermittent *E*mployee - game which was required of most (*not all*) newly assigned correctional officers.

In order for me to work my desired 40-hour week, I (along with other newbes) was required to call-in and make myself available to fill-in behind short-notice cancellations. Although bothersome, this process was somewhat effective and it allowed me to consistently work a 40-hour week. Like many of the other newbes, I was unable to secure any continuity in my life, as I couldn't make any personal plans. On occasions, I would work two back-to-back watches (16-hour shifts), without any consideration for overtime.

Fortunately, for the great majority of us, our *PIE*-status terminated after 90 days, and we all then became fully bonafide permanent staff. Unfortunately, for me, that process merely involved a transition from something undesirable to something less undesirable.

Many of my former correctional officer academy classmates were now earmarked for permanent job and watch assignments. However, I merely became, in essence, a permanent *VR* (vacation relief) correctional officer; which meant that I was plugged into a slot (that varied from all three watches/shifts) when a correctional officer took vacation.

There were many advantages in my working *VR*. For instance, I became thoroughly knowledgeable and proficient in most positions required of a correctional officer at Folsom.

My experience and knowledge are more aptly expressed by a situation which occurred in which a *seasoned* correctional officer, wanting overtime pay, was asked to work in the dining facility.

Unfortunately, that officer had neither the experience nor the training to take charge and motivate the head cook (an inmate) to begin preparing the breakfast meal.

The Watch Sergeant, having been aware of my knowledge and past performances in other areas of Folsom, personally contacted me and asked that I, "switch" positions with the other officer to insure that the meal would be prepared on time.

When I arrived in the dining room, several inmates were lying on tables and literally *clowning* the officer who had no clue in effectively handling the situation.

I immediately took charge which resulted in the meal being prepared and served on time. That's merely one situation that occurred in which my knowledge of the respective areas within Folsom became very useful. In my opinion, that is a positive for Vacation Relief.

One of the negative factors, however, prohibits continuity in any given position; thereby, failing to provide either the Watch Lieutenant or Watch Sergeant with an accurate assessment of one's consistent work performance.

I wasn't at Folsom 90 days when a very high ranking uniformed (not to be confused with *uninformed*) staff member observed me exiting the institution with my uniform coat on, minus a tie.

Now, to most of you, the immediate response would be, "So what?" However, this individual decided to take issue with the fact that I was not in compliance with uniform standards (that required the use of a tie when the coat was worn) even though I was exiting the institution.

What alarmed me most of all, wasn't the fact that my *breach* of uniform standards was brought to my attention; rather, it was the negative manner in which the individual approached me. That *approach* netted the following typed response from me on the same day of occurrence and delivered to that individual:

"Captain Blair: Sir, I am the Officer[that] you stopped (outside the Administration Building) this morning and offered what was supposed to be constructive criticism.

I would be sorely remiss if I failed to inform you that what you offered may have been criticism, but it certainly wasn't constructive.

In my opinion, you lacked both tact and discretion and your lack of effective communication skills left much to be desired.

Captain, I am not the enemy and I refuse to allow you or anyone in the System to talk down to me.

You were not only extremely abrasive but, your professional conduct toward me and Sergeant Burns was absolutely abhorrent.

Although Sergeant Burns did not share his personal sentiments with me, I was embarrassed for him.

Forgive me for my naiveté, but I am unaccustomed in watching my superior belittled by his superior in my presence.

Incidentally, had you taken a moment to fully assess the situation, you would have noted that Sergeant Burns was about fifteen paces to my rear and could not have possibly seen that I was not wearing a tie.

Captain, although you didn't take the time to ask me if I had a good Watch, I will share this with you ... I reported for work with less than a three-hour notification and, without benefit of having time to bring a sandwich with me.

iN tHE cAR

Now, while I don't expect any pat on the back, I do expect ... no, I demand to be treated like a professional and team-player that I am.

Captain, now that I've shared my thoughts with you, let's put this incident behind us and get on with the business at hand -- safeguarding our staff, the institution, our inmates, and the general public."

Sincerely, Lonnie F. DeWitt (cc: Warden Blue)

Wild rumors immediately began to circulate around Folsom from, "that young punk, just driving up and already on the Captain's shit list!" To, "DeWitt is either crazy or he has a lot of guts." The **truth** is probably hidden somewhere between those two rumors.

By their very nature, correctional institutions create and maintain a cesspool of rumors. It didn't take very long for the name, "DeWitt" to be heard all over Folsom (both old and new).

I had an occasion for a Correctional Sergeant to approach me and comment (with an obvious sigh of non-verbal disapproval), "Oh! So, you're DeWitt!" **Yes, I'm DeWitt**.

My definition of **r-e-s-p-e-c-t** is when two or more people find it necessary to combine their efforts in a covert attempt to orchestrate a negative outcome against another. To me, that's **r-e-s-p-e-c-t** (albeit *cowardly*) because it clearly shows that: (1) individually, each person felt powerless to effect his/her desired negative outcome; (2) that it took the collective efforts of two or more people to either effect or attempt to effect that negative outcome; and, (3) the conspirators found it necessary to operate in absolute silence and secrecy. To me, that's **r-e-s-p-e-c-t**.

I later learned that managers and supervisors within the California Department of Corrections routinely operate in *a mode of secrecy* and in a *conspiracy of silence* to cover-up their illegal and unethical actions.

There is an unfortunate mindset within CDC where *tolerance is oftentimes confused with acceptance.* Like most professional team players, I prefer to be fully accepted into an organization and valued for my individuality.

It is absolutely inconceivable, to me, for anyone to either expect or demand respect and not reciprocate. Whatever happened to the *old-fashion* ideology of fully accepting and respecting someone *unconditionally*?

How can one (logically) expect me to respect someone (or, an institution) where I have been systematically excluded from its inner-circles? While I window shop and peer in from the outside, others are on the inside (of the car) making critical decisions affecting my career progression (or, digression).

By design, neither my gold nor my platinum plastic card would allow me unlimited and unobtrusive access within CDC's inner circles.

How can I then be asked to become subordinate to and respect an environment that offers nothing short of intellectual deceit and clearly lacks self-respect?

R-e-s-p-e-c-t, therefore, cuts much deeper than a double-edge sword. In order to achieve respect, *we must*:

> **R**ely on
> **E**veryone's
> **S**trengths to effect a
> **P**ositive outcome in our
> **E**nvironment while we
> **C**ollectively involve and integrate each person as a
> **T**eam player

I simply refuse to have my innovativeness stymied because of the outward lack of respect that most CDC managers give to minority staff.

I predict that this outward contempt for human dignity and decency will be the eventual demise of the California Department of

Corrections (as we know it today).

I am reminded of a poem (author unknown) that I received while attending the Parole Agent Academy that closely mirrors CDC's true reflections and my prediction for its ultimate demise:

"THE COLD WITHIN"

*Six humans trapped by happenstance
in dark and bitter cold.
Each one possessed a stick of wood;
or, so the story's told.
Their dying fire in need of logs,
The first woman held hers back;
for of the faces around the fire,
she noticed one was black.
The next man looking 'cross the way
saw one not of his church,
And couldn't bring himself to give
The fire his stick of birch.
The third one sat in tattered clothes.
He gave his coat a hitch.
Why should his log be put to use
To warm the idle rich?
The black man's face bespoke revenge
as the fire passed from sight;
For all he saw in his stick of wood
Was a chance to spite the white.
The last man of this forlorn group
Did naught except for gain.
Giving only to those who gave
Was how he played the game.
The logs held tight in death's still hands
Was proof of human sin.
They didn't die from the cold without.
They died from the cold within.*

So it is with many (*not all*) of our California Department of Corrections managers and supervisors who will, undoubtedly, find an agonizing *death* - (spiritually, emotionally, and possibly even physically) from *The Cold Within* - simply because they either refused or lacked the capacity and intellect to ***do the right thing***.

Chapter Nine

A Volley of Set-ups

Well, here we go again. Another *seasoned* correctional staff attempted to *clown* me that necessitated the following official response from Lieutenant Snitzer:

"On January 20, 1990, at approximately 2330 hours, Correctional Officer L. DeWitt was *reported to be acting in an unprofessional manner by making disrespectful statements to and insubordination. Reports were taken from five (5) officers and two (2) sergeants involved and submitted to Correctional Captain Blair for appropriate Administrative Review and Action."*

Of course, I was required to make a statement that evening, which is included below:

January 20, 1990

"STATEMENT OF FACTS"

On January 20, 1990, at approximately 2330 (1130 P.M.), while relieving Third Watch, I backed vehicle #50 and drove forward about five feet when I realized that the Sign-Out Sheets (normally given to me by the Third Watch Sergeant/Lieutenant) weren't available, as they are customarily placed on the center van receptacle.

I then stopped the vehicle and asked Sergeant Russell, Third Watch Sergeant, if he had brought the sheets. He replied that he hadn't and that I could simply drop them off later. I replied, "OK" and as I began to drive off, Officer Fowler shouted, "Close my fucking door and let's get out of here!" I then responded, "That's my fucking door not yours -- I have the keys."

Officer Fowler and I then had an exchange of unpleasantness and finally, I simply told him to, "Shut the fuck up!" He uttered something to the effect that he would shut up, but ... (implied that I'll hear from him again). He then said something about a, "...Rookie just driving up with only six months in the Department..." I corrected him and said, "five months." Again, I repeated that he, "Just shut *the fuck*

iN tHE cAR

up!"

Sergeant Russell then interceded; however, he addressed only me and stated his disapproval of my asking Officer Fowler to shut up. Not once did Sergeant Russell express his dissatisfaction with Officer Fowler, giving the appearance that I was totally at fault and that Officer Fowler was completely exonerated from our verbal confrontation. Sergeant Russell then said something about my, "negative attitude;" however, he failed to acknowledge that Officer Fowler was not only the other party to a fair exchange of unpleasantness, but that Officer Fowler was the initiator!

Sergeant Russell asked me to pull the vehicle over which I complied and he began to literally counsel me with a van full of other officers. I then suggested to Sergeant Russell that he and I could take our conversation elsewhere. Sergeant Russell immediately asked, "Are you threatening me?" I answered that I was not threatening him and that I merely meant that he and I could discuss my "attitude" in a more appropriate setting (minus the audience).

It apparently took Captain Blair and Sergeant Russell nearly three months to decide that I should receive a Letter of Instruction (LOI), (which is equivalent to a letter of reprimand). Again, this action necessitated the following response from me:

Dear Warden:

During my 7-month tenure at Folsom I have fully supported you and your policies both on and off the institution. Now, I would like to see some of that support channeled downward (to me).

On March 30, I received a Letter of Instruction from Sergeant Russell who made the following comment to me:

"I have been directed by Captain Blair to give you this Letter of Instruction."

Now, notwithstanding the fact that this LOI came as a complete surprise to me - 68 days after the incident occurred - since I was never advised that I would receive one.

Furthermore, apparently your staff has elected to violate the Agreement between the State of California and California Correctional Peace Officers' Association covering Bargaining Unit 6.

Specifically, paragraph 9.06 Letters of Instructions states:

"b. Letters of Instructions/WIDS shall be written in a timely fashion; generally within thirty (30) days from when the incident occurred or from date of discovery of the incident that forms the basis for the LOI or WID. Unless special circumstances exist, LOIs or WIDs should not be written if the knowledge of the incident is more than thirty (30) days old."

Warden, be advised, I am not one to hide behind any technicality. Hopefully, upon your reading my letter, you will agree with me that the contents of the LOI are absolutely without merit!

You may also have cause to question the motives of your staff - are their motives really professional or, perhaps personal? The LOI (dated March 26th) that I acknowledged on March 30th had Captain Blair's teeth prints all over it -- could it possibly be an adolescent display of vindictiveness over my November 6, 1989 letter to him?

Warden, I would much rather use my energies more constructively than playing these childish "I gotcha games!"

The night of the incident in question (January 20th), I was interviewed by Lieutenants Schellington and Rollin. It wasn't until after I had written my statement (not that it mattered) that I was advised of the, "serious allegations" against me.

When I first sat down, Lt. Schellington looked at me and stated: "I think you have an attitude problem!" My reply to him was simply, "Lieutenant, you don't know me well enough to make that statement." Shortly afterwards, both lieutenants left making these departing remarks (witnessed by on-duty staff):

iN tHE cAR

Lt. Schellington
"I just won't tolerate it....someone just driving up and thinks he has something coming."
Lt. Rollin
"DeWitt is out of here...he's through!"

On February 3, 1990 at approximately 0130, I had an official inquiry with both Lieutenants Schellington and Rollin (again); however, at that time, both appeared to be more receptive (and even apologetic) and both agreed that they could easily see where there was a misunderstanding between Sergeant Russell and me as opposed to the alleged charges.

Warden, I personally considered the "*official inquiry*" as a form of reconciliatory since (in my opinion) both lieutenants had previously biased themselves in this incident. However, quite honestly, I was neither concerned nor apprehensive during the interview since both appeared to have made a 180-degree turn since their initial interview with me.

Warden, where is the breakdown? Both lieutenants agreed with me and I have spoken to one of the officers in the van who also agreed that there was neither a threat nor insubordination.

Warden, hopefully, you will also agree with me that this issue has been botched and blown greatly out of proportion since the (inappropriate) AOD Memorandum was issued on 1/21/90!

I contacted Lieutenant Daniels on April 10, 1990 (per Sergeant Russell's instructions) to obtain a copy of the LOI. Lt. Daniels informed me that the LOI contained "*incorrect data*" and that it was currently being rewritten for reissuing by Sergeant Russell.

Warden, it certainly doesn't take a microscopic review for one to determine that this entire incident reeks with irregularities and inconsistencies.

For instance, <u>that</u> LOI charged me with driving in an unsafe manner that caused a threat to my passengers and myself.

However, the record will indicate that not once was my driving an issue! When does this proliferation of "*issues*" stop - when I receive my, "*corrected*" LOI?

Warden, it's significant to note that since this alleged "incident" I have been personally asked by no less than two sergeants and one lieutenant to permanently work for them. It's also extremely gratifying to know that we have at least one sergeant at Folsom who has the capacity to objectively and accurately evaluate, record, and report a subordinate's performance as reflected by the overall "Outstanding" rating given me on my Report of Performance for Probationary Employee (enclosed) which covered the time frame during which the alleged "incident" occurred. And, yes, the rater was fully aware of the incident.

Warden, if you agree with me, please have all documents pertaining to this incident destroyed. However, if you honestly believe that your staff acted in good faith and you fully support their actions, then I must request copies of all statements, correspondence, memorandums, etc., be given to me, pursuant to the Freedom of Information Act.

As in the past, I will close this letter with a positive note. Warden, I am writing you this letter because I trust you and I trust that you will do what's right. If you wish to share the contents of this letter with anyone, obviously, that's your prerogative. However, rest assured that my copy would go no further than my review if justice were served.

I realize that an LOI is merely administrative; however, I will not accept it if it's unwarranted - as in this instance.

Warden, I realize that you have a very busy schedule; however, if you are unclear about anything that I've said or, if you merely wish to talk with me, I'd certainly appreciate it. My schedule follows: [**My Work schedule was included in the original letter**]

In closing, Warden, I ask that you consider the merits of this entire incident. Given my past (23 years of) military discipline is it really conceivable that I would threaten a superior (and in the presence of other officers)? I think not.

During my military career I have given many lectures/speeches and there is one thought I'd like to leave with you:

iN tHE cAR 75

> *"In the social order in which one person is subordinate to another, the superior, if he is a gentleman, never speaks of it; the subordinate, if he is a gentleman, never forgets it!"*
>
> (General Pershing)

Your staff does not have to either flex their muscles or toot their horns for me to know that they have them....I am a gentleman and I will automatically render respect to an elder and to a superior. But, as we are both well aware, respect is a double-edged sword!

Sincerely, Lonnie F. DeWitt

Whew! What a letter! Well, needless to say, that *set-up* failed, as I did not receive any kind of administrative/adverse action. There was quite some humor to this entire episode; especially, when I confronted Sergeant Russell and asked, "Why are you **proliferating** these issues?" I knew that the Sergeant was clueless and had no idea what the word, **"proliferating"** meant; however, I merely wanted to watch him squirm and attempt to conceal his ignorance (which is exactly what he did)!

The Warden and I did have an occasion - in passing - to briefly discuss this incident. At that time, he cautioned me by saying, "You need to be more careful in knowing some of the people you are dealing with." I answered. "Yes, I do; and, they also need to be more careful in dealing with me!"

Incidentally, the *only* correctional officer (in the van) who had the courage and integrity to objectively and accurately report what had really happened was a former Vietnamese military officer.

Isn't life filled with irony? *I spent one year and two days helping him fight for his country's freedom. Now, more than two decades later, he is in America helping me fight for mine!*

On May 8, 1990, during an evening meal, a Black inmate (later identified as Gary) asked permission to speak with me following the meal. As one of the two floor officers, assigned to that inmate's housing unit in *B-Facility*, I told him that I would call him out of his *house* (cell) upon completion of the meal (once the other inmates were locked up).

When I returned to my position in the dining room, the other floor officer, Officer Evers, asked me who the inmate was. I stated that I did not know his name; however, that I did have his *house number* since the inmate wanted to speak with me later. Officer Evers then walked away and conversed with the Facility Sergeant.

Upon returning, Officer Evers then asked me, "Did you see that inmate [Gary] *eye-fucking* me?" I stated that I didn't. I had no idea what, *"eye-fucking"* meant. But, I later wondered if it held the same meaning as the old, *"roving eyeballs"* allegations (of the Deep South) where Black men and Black boys were dragged out of their homes and either beaten to death or lynched for allegedly *looking* at a White woman or White girl). I then stated that I would be calling the inmate into the office later because he (the inmate) had asked to speak with me. Officer Evers then replied that *he* would be calling the inmate into the office.

Afterwards, Officer Evers asked the Control Officer (gunner) to unlock the inmate's door. When the inmate entered the office, Officer Evers motioned the inmate to sit down, which he complied. The conversation went like this:

Officer Evers
"Do you remember me?"
Inmate Gary
Nodded, affirmatively.
Officer Evers
"Well, I remember you, too. Weren't you in (another part of Folsom), and didn't you say that you were going to kick my ass? You were a liar then, and you're a liar now!"
Inmate Gary
"Officer, I don't want any trouble. I'll just go back to my house."

iN tHE cAR

At that point, Inmate Gary stood up in an effort to leave the office; however, Officer Evers stepped in front of Inmate Gary and cautioned the inmate not to leave the office until he (Officer Evers) told him to do so.

Inmate Gary then raised both arms to accommodate a clothed body search (although, Officer Evers had not indicated that was his intentions). However, Officer Evers did, at that point, command Inmate Gary to, "face the wall."

Inmate Gary complied, placing both hands (palms flat) against the wall. Officer Evers then (with his right hand) grabbed Inmate Gary's waistline and repeatedly kicked Inmate Gary's inner left foot, which caused Inmate Gary to significantly widen his stance.

After several minutes of cursing and degrading Inmate Gary, Officer Evers then advised Inmate Gary that, "in ten seconds" he (Officer Evers) would give Inmate Gary the, "opportunity" to walk out of the office.

After about ten seconds, Officer Evers then ordered Inmate Gary to, "sit down" and discuss with me the reason(s) for his initial request. Inmate Gary simply replied, "Never mind!"

Officer Evers then directed the inmate to leave the office and return *home*. Inmate Gary departed the office, without further incident.

About fifteen minutes later, Inmate Gary sent a *kite* (a complaint form), by one of the inmate tier workers, to Officer Evers. Upon reading the document, Officer Evers then crumpled and threw the document into the trash can. However, a few seconds later, Officer Evers then withdrew the document from the trash can and stated to me, "Can you believe this shit; (holding up the crumpled document) you gotta back me up on this!"

I then advised Officer Evers that he did not want me to comment on that scenario, as anything that I would offer would certainly hurt him!

After about a week of denying the incident to the Facility Lieutenant, Officer Evers (tearfully) admitted his wrongdoing. To my knowledge, there was no action taken against Officer Evers; and he never forgave me for not, *"backing"* his *play*.

On June 8, 1990, at approximately 8:10 A.M., I saw Inmate Gary in the *A-Facility* X-ray unit. At that time, he told me that he had been in the Security Housing Unit (SHU) since the incident because, "they said I threatened staff." How bogus (yet, typical)!

The big joke in *B-Facility* was working with Officer Evers, who looked shorter than a legal midget. Staff knew that Officer Evers suffered from a *short man's* complex; and that he was known to do something *stupid*; thereby, endangering the lives of other staff.

Consequently, officers who either worked with Officer Evers, or alongside him, would breathe a comical sigh of relief when the Watch was over.

On September 2, 1991, I was one of two officers assigned to *C-2 Facility Control.* In this capacity, the other officer and I were responsible for providing gun coverage for the two officers on the floor and for the inmates assigned to the housing unit.

On this particular day, the two officers entered two vacant *homes* of inmates, while conducting routine housing searches. Upon completion of these two searches, one of the officers then pulled two cassette tapes from between his shirt and undershirt.

I did not know if the tapes belonged to the officer (who chose an inappropriate time to *secret* these items from inside his shirt); or, if the officer had taken the tape from the inmates' quarters. It was, however, against policy for staff to bring contraband (which included cassette tapes) into the prison.

After fully discussing the incident and analyzing possible options with the other Control officer, I then contacted the Facility Sergeant.

When the Facility Sergeant arrived, I informed him of my observations. After the Sergeant and the officer discussed the matter, the Sergeant told me, "he's a *good wood*" (which meant that the officer was a, *"peckerwood in good standings"*) - a term commonly used by white staff to describe either a White staff or White inmate in a prison setting.

A, *"good wood." Good* by whose standards? What yardstick was used to *determine* that this man was a, *"good wood?"*

At this point, I offer no answers; I only have questions.

The Sergeant went on to say that the tapes belonged to the officer who was verbally cautioned regarding CDC policy which prohibited staff from bringing personal items of that nature into a correctional institution.

I had several concerns, which I shared with the other Control Officer prior to notifying the Facility Sergeant. One of my concerns was that the officer had (possibly) brought contraband into a prison. I felt that by my confronting the Officer he would either lie or tell me to mind my own business. Another concern was that the Officer possibly stole the items from an inmate's house, which could cause immediate retaliation against other unsuspecting officers and quickly escalate into an extremely serious and uncontrollable situation. At the very minimum, if theft were involved, increased distrust and animosity between inmates and staff would be visibly evident.

Immediately after the Facility Sergeant left, the Floor Officer asked me if I had told. I replied that I had and, I shared my concerns with the Officer. I then asked the Officer had I asked him about the cassette tapes, what would have been his response. He replied, "I would have told you to mind your own business!"

After this incident, and while at Folsom, I received several harassing and anonymous telephone calls (like the individual who telephoned me and simply said, *"snitch"* and then hung up). How juvenile!

By then, the word had gotten out that, **"DeWitt won't back your play."** *No, I won't, "back your play;"* especially, when you're playing the wrong tune *(offbeat)*.

Unfortunately, that's the price we pay when we hire *kids*, with *restricted mentalities* and *misguided loyalties*, to do a grown-up's job.

Some of these impressionable little children actually *idolize* the very people that they are charged to supervise. These *officers* are deprived of those *warm fuzzies* at home; consequently, they rely on their extended families - inmates - to help fill that void.

While all children need (positive) role models, many **correctional adolescents** are emotionally impoverished which literally compels them to become psychotic leeches to the Stockholm Syndrome.

The *whispering campaign* continues.

Chapter Ten

Professionally Unprofessional

To me, it seems as though all (or most) of the managers, whose employment is with the California Department of Corrections, are engulfed in a blinding fog of total insecurity which demands that:

*"For most personnel actions,
management is systematically obligated
to render a negative reaction!"*

Even the most mundane and extremely simple personnel action requests are met with negative and oftentimes harsh management decisions. CDC managers give the appearance that they resent its staff from *officially* requesting *anything* in writing.

It appears more *acceptable* for staff to *verbally request* a personnel action; therefore, if managers choose not to reply, they are not obligated to *officially* respond.

However, once that request becomes documented, in writing, then management not only feels intimidated by having to respond but, more importantly, management must then garner its mentally restrictive resources to provide an *administratively adequate* (politically correct) yet, oftentimes, negative response.

When I out-processed Folsom, after being *promoted* to a parole agent, I complained to the Associate Warden about the unprofessional and degrading treatment that I received from the Assignment Lieutenant. That lieutenant had, on two separate occasions, hung the telephone up in my face and did not give me the courtesy of out-processing the institution on State time (as required by directives). The Associate Warden's reply to me was simply, "You wouldn't have these problems if you learn to make friends!"

By that comment, one can easily see why CDC gets a failing grade, from me, in communication skills. A course in Sensitivity 101 would also be in order. It's truly unfortunate that we do not possess the capability to *retrofit* some managers employed within the California Department of Corrections with sensitivity or, at least, common sense.

This cadre of *self-righteous manly men* seem to stand in line as they share recycled sanitary napkins with which to powder puff their snotty noses. One may easily understand and even appreciate how I could very easily become a staunch proponent of *retroactive abortion.*

The Department's management staff has once again shown that it is, and will probably continue to be, professionally unprofessional. If an Associate Warden has that kind of simpleton mentality, it is reasonable to expect prison staff to emulate the boss. That particular (former) Associate Warden was demoted to a correctional officer for either his illicit involvement with or his repeated sexual harassment of a female correctional staff (an all *too frequent* occurrence within the California Department of Corrections). Could this possibly be a *learned response* that this correctional idiot imitated from his boss?

The citizens of California pay an inordinate price tag (which, unfortunately, equates to more than just money) to keep these *wannabe* managers employed.

An enormously internal power struggle exists within the California Department of Corrections that creates a constant turmoil which leaves many defenseless victims (staff, inmates and parolees) in its wake.

When I was first assigned as a parole agent to the Race Street Parole Office, I was very fortunate to work for a very professional supervisor, Sally Aguirre, in Unit 6. Ms. Aguirre's daily demeanor and objectivity were clearly evident and appreciated by all of her subordinates. It was standard procedure for the entire staff to openly communicate, address and share common issues with her and with each other.

In fact, Ms. Aguirre told me that if I did a, "good job" for her that she would recommend my reassignment, "in about a year" to Sacramento for me to be with my family.

Unfortunately, our unit was deactivated and all of our personnel were scattered throughout the Race Street office and the parole office on Lewis Road. Both offices are in San Jose.

I was told that all of the other unit supervisors wanted me to work for them because of the excellent evaluation rating that I received from Ms. Aguirre and her positive comments about me to the other unit supervisors.

However, because Mr. Curtis Jackson (*CJ*) - a *Black* senior supervisor - had first choice, I was, unfortunately, his choice.

I had heard several bad rumors about *CJ* and how he, "screwed over" a young Black female parole agent. This agent eventually failed the mandatory probationary period and was subsequently returned to her former position as a correctional officer.

Several parole agents and supervisors would laugh and openly comment that, "*CJ* was anal retentive!" I was determined not to let those rumors and negative comments detract from my own thirst for knowledge and perfection within the parole community.

At the onset of my assignment to Unit 5, it became immediately apparent to me that *CJ* suffered from some serious and deep-rooted emotional problems that did not permit him to manage with either empathy or compassion. *CJ* was (CDC) book-wise; however, he lacked common sense. The sign that *CJ* proudly displayed on his office wall most aptly expressed that kind of sick and morbid mindset:

**There's No Reason For It–
It's Just Our Policy!"**

Mr. Jackson was *right*, of course, since oftentimes there were no logical reason(s) for management to make certain decisions. Unfortunately, once those decisions were made, they became *policy*.

"So it is written...so it shall be done!"

As with most bureaucratic organizations, managers tend to view passiveness as the accepted standards. Therefore, *proactive* individuals are easily *singled out* and eventually *eliminated*, if they are **not** *iN tHE cAR*.

For instance, working through one's lunch hour is generally frowned upon by many managers - not because of union issues but - because those kinds of positive traits often identify individuals who are clearly head and shoulders above the rest.

Unfortunately, CDC managers simply cannot swallow that kind of (positive) image projected by a minority who is **not** *iN tHE cAR*.

It was not uncommon for me to work twelve- to fourteen-hour days (without any expectations of overtime payment consideration, as there was none). Other parole agents would jokingly tell me to, "Get a life" because I was *almost always* the first agent in the office in the mornings and usually the last person to leave in the evenings.

During the weekdays I enjoyed working *overtime* because it gave me the opportunity to critically examine my case files and to closely monitor and adhere to monthly reporting and other administrative requirements.

On Fridays, however, I seldom worked past four o'clock (unless I was required to work a weekend) because I usually headed for home - Sacramento - a one-way distance of 130 miles.

As a newly appointed parole agent in Unit 6, Ms. Aguirre gave me the opportunity and additional experience by serving as both (Acting) Unit Supervisor (US) and (Acting) Assistant Unit Supervisor (AUS).

Although *CJ* asked and allowed another junior parole agent (who I graduated with from the Parole Academy) to serve in those capacities, he *never* offered me that opportunity.

Even my performance evaluations suffered because *CJ* severely lacked the capacity to rate (*me*) objectively. I challenged him on one such report. My written comments to the South Bay Field Parole Administrator, Steve Scheller were:

Dear Mr. Scheller:

I respectfully request that my recent Report of Performance for Probationary Employee be rewritten by Mr. Jackson to reflect a more accurate assessment of my work performance. I believe that Mr. Jackson has mistakenly used my final probationary evaluation as a counseling tool.

If dissatisfied with the quality of my work (that is reflected in the word picture of my evaluation), why didn't Mr. Jackson simply counsel me verbally and follow-up in writing, if his verbal counseling failed to achieve the desired results? Throughout the report, Mr. Jackson mentions my work on the computer in a negative manner. In fact, he stated, "I have mentioned this to you several times. However, you continue to do your reports on the computer." The comment regarding my using the computer is true; however, the other comment is untrue."

This subject was clearly addressed and remedied (I thought) during one of our Unit meetings. Mr. Jackson, at that time, expressed his dissatisfaction with agents using the computer vs. writing/transcribing reports. However, our AUS initiated a "rebuttal" stating that because of his excellent typing skills, he would prefer using the computer to draft his reports. I agreed with the AUS, adding that my writing was so poor that I was oftentimes asked to type my signature!

While at this meeting, Mr. Jackson relinquished his initial position and stated that he would allow Agents, who so desired, to use the computer to type reports. To my knowledge, Mr. Jackson did not change his (relinquished) position until I read my evaluation report.

Mr. Scheller, please note that I spent eight of my twelve probationary months in Unit #6 without difficulty and interestingly noteworthy, without a single report being returned for correction.

Conversely, my last four probationary months in my current Unit has found me "correcting" virtually every report that I've written.

Mr. Scheller, my proven abilities to make sound and decisive decisions have consistently culminated in positive results. Furthermore, I enjoy the reputation at Race Street of being a total team player.

Although I disagree with Mr. Jackson's comments that dictating my reports "will be quicker" (I type 80 wpm); however, I have no objections to either dictating or writing drafts. However, (I am certain that you will agree with me that) this must be articulated to me through other than an evaluation report.

To Mr. Jackson's credit, I must state that he has brought several valid observations to my attention that will certainly assist me as I grow into a "seasoned" Agent.

Unless I'm otherwise advised, however, I view my supervisor's comments (along with those offered by other senior Agents) as valuable and constructive criticism that, as an Apprentice, I expect to periodically receive. I was unaware that Mr. Jackson viewed his casual comments as a form of "counseling."

When I was assigned to Unit #5, my caseload (count) greatly exceeded the regulatory case count; and, for a few months I carried the highest case count in Unit #5, that included felons and non-felons.

Like most agents, I absorbed my additional workload without complaint. It was customary for me to consistently work a 10- to 12-hour day. A request for overtime was neither an issue then nor is it an issue now. I'm only stating facts.

Throughout this period (that included a tremendous surge in caseloads) many specifications were waived in order for us to maximize our time. I will offer you verbal comments to my evaluation that, "Two cases had no field calls; one for 27 days and the other for 51 days."

Hopefully, upon my oral presentation, you will agree that I exercised sound judgment in each case.

As a student from the "old school", I take pride identifying with my supervisor's list of priorities in order to be of greater value to him/her. Consequently, his/her priorities become my priorities.

While I once believed that I was "on track" with Mr. Jackson now, I am totally confused. I believed, at the time, that Mr. Jackson's priorities were given to timely BPT actions and Discharge Reviews (to eliminate/minimize "Discharges by Operational Law"). My records clearly reflect that I had "zero" "By Law" discharges (where I failed to submit a timely discharge review during my entire 12-month probationary period).

Similarly, I take pride in my timely submission of BPT reports. Again, my records will indicate a 98% timely rate on all my BPT reports; and, the remaining 2% could clearly stand the closest scrutiny of explanation.

Mr. Scheller, I am confident that once you consider the merits of both my written and oral presentations that you will concur with my request to have my evaluation rewritten.

Sincerely, Lonnie F. DeWitt

By my being very candid, obviously, had a negative impact. On May 10, 1993, *CJ* and I had a meeting with Steve in an effort to resolve my contention that *CJ* had *mistakenly* used my final probationary evaluation as a counseling tool. Prior to our meeting, Steve told *CJ*, "You have an unhappy camper." (Obviously, referring to me).

At that time, several issues were addressed; however, none were amicably resolved (to my satisfaction). *CJ's* mindset, however, was of immediate concern to me. In the presence of Steve, when I asked *CJ* to simply, "rate me objectively," he replied: *'Since we don't work on an assembly line making 'widgets' where our production could be objectively measured by numbers, I will continue to be a subjective rater. That's my management style!"*

I simply could not believe what *CJ* said. I recognized that *CJ* was not very bright; however, a relatively old and widely used technique called Management By Objective (MBO) was available, in the library, for him to *polish* his management skills. When used, this management tool offers *objectivity* in evaluating individual and group performances.

Of course, given the extremely remote chance that he asked, I would have been more than willing to offer him the benefit of my education and past experiences as a manager. However, consider the odds (of his asking).

Another issue, which caused me concern, was *CJ's* position that he considered it *counseling* every time he interacted with his employees - even in a training mode. Again, this was verbally expressed in the presence of Steve. It's truly unfortunate that *CJ* simply could not share the wealth of his knowledge and experiences with his subordinates, in a training mode, without his having to scurry back to his desk and document the event as *counseling*.

During the initial draft of my letter to Steve, I had asked that he, "...seriously consider my transfer from Unit #5 to either Unit #1 or a Unit at Lewis Road." However, I decided not to pursue that (transfer) option, which I later regretted.

I also believed that *CJ* suffered from selective amnesia. For instance, I had been commended by several Unit Supervisors and Acting Unit Supervisors who had occasions to review my written reports. *CJ*, however, failed to recognize, appreciate, or comment on my writing skills. But, he made it a point to address the, "excellent" writing skills of other agents in their evaluation reports.

During my oral presentation with Steve, I mentioned the fact that *CJ* had me *correcting* virtually every report that I wrote, which was a major source of concern with our clerical staff. I was required to change an entire report because *CJ corrected* my grammar. That report went out grammatically incorrect simply to humor *CJ*.

The joke in Unit 5 was that, "DeWitt had to virtually chop down an entire forest to make one minor change to a report!"

Another Unit 5 joke was, "Well, at least I'm not Black!" (A White female parole agent would frequently tell me that, in reference to the obvious unequal treatment and negative attention that *CJ* unrelentingly showed me). *CJ* was a self-made **jester!**

The full impact of that quoted parole agent became more meaningful when I later learned that *CJ* had privately shared his *philosophy* with a Black parole agent:

> "I expect us (Blacks) to work twice as hard as Whites and receive half the credit."

That kind of slavery-time mentality fully captures the true essence of *CJ's real* mindset and *unfortunate philosophy*. His *character* is closely mirrored in this *imaginary statement*, which I suspect he would have made during America's darkest hours:

> "Gimme 'da whip boss; 'ol Unk'l CJ uh keep 'em in line!"

The California Department of, "What?!" How dare we say, "Corrections!"

How can one reasonably expect the Department to *correct* the behavior of its inmates and parolees when it consistently hire, promote, and condone such negative behavior from its own staff, including its managers?

Actually, I began to wonder about the integrity of our entire law enforcement family. I had the occasion to assist the San Jose Police Department's narcotics enforcement team (NET) in a parole search of one of my parolee's residence. The team had (confidential) information regarding the alleged drug sales by one of my parolees. Although my parolee's entire criminal record reflected numerous arrests for personal drug use (not sales), it was customary for law enforcement agencies to extend professional courtesy to each other.

Consequently, when I briefed the team (which also included a parole agent-NET coordinator), I drew a rough diagram of the parolee's home and indicated which room was considered *off-limits* for parole search purposes.

Since the parolee lived with his brother, the brother's room was, therefore, deemed *off-limits*.

When we arrived at the location, the parolee took too long to answer the door; therefore, we made a keyless entry. Upon entering the residence, my parolee was immediately handcuffed. There were no other occupants in the home.

While I was talking with the parolee, I heard one of the police officers say, "Let's just say we smelled marijuana." At that point, I asked another officer to watch my parolee while I looked in the rear of the home, where the bedrooms were located.

To my disbelief, the officers had entered the *off-limits* bedroom, which had been *locked from the outside*! I saw several weapons and an item that appeared to be an incendiary device, which the officers had placed on the bed.

The officers *then* requested and received a Search Warrant. **Wrong**! Any self-respecting police officer will tell you that a clear Constitutional Rights violation had occurred. Furthermore, the officers who requested and subsequently received the Search Warrant to enter a room, which had already been entered into, did so, feloniously.

I had problems with that. When I confronted the on-scene parole agent-NET coordinator and expressed my disapproval of this illegal search, this parole agent would only say that he, "liked going out with them [NET members] because they bought lunch for everybody."

It then became obvious that *integrity* had now been reduced to a cheeseburger, small fries and a medium soft drink. I wondered how much this parole agent would have *sacrificed* for a ***supersized meal!***

The narcotic enforcement team leader then asked that I arrest my parolee (to somehow *validate* the parole search, the illegal entry and subsequent illegal search warrant). I refused. There was no overwhelming reason to justify my parolee's *immediate* incarceration.

I believed that my parolee had recently used drugs; however, he posed no immediate threat to the community, as he had no history of violence. Besides, I also knew that my parolee's mom had just arrived in San Jose from out-of-State and that she was currently visiting other relatives.

I told my parolee, "I'm giving you two days to visit with your mother; then, I want you to self-surrender to me." He agreed.

When I mentioned this incident to my supervisor, *CJ*, he simply said, "Well, if you're called to testify, you know that you have to tell the truth." Of course, I had to, "tell the truth." But, that really wasn't the issue. There was clearly a much bigger issue; and if *CJ* missed it, shame on him. No, *CJ **did not** miss* that issue. He simply refused to address it. Double shame on him.

Sadly, *CJ* wasn't at all either interested in or concerned with that illegal search. He was more focused on the fact that I didn't call him and let him make the decision on whether or not I should have arrested my parolee. *CJ* made it quite clear that I should have, "favored on the side of conservatism" and arrested my parolee. Yes, *CJ* was upset because I didn't give him the opportunity to exercise *his,* "styles of managing" *(subjective and micro)*.

On the second day following that incident, my parolee self-surrendered (as agreed) and subsequently completed a 30-day drug detoxification program.

Sometimes later, the Public Defender for my parolee's brother telephoned me and I essentially told him that the search warrant to enter into that room was inappropriately (illegally) obtained.

The District Attorney then sent one of his Assistants to speak with me. I told the Assistant District Attorney exactly what I told the Public Defender. He wasn't very pleased with what I had to say. In fact, he attempted to place me on the defensive by asking me, "What is your relationship with your parolees?" I laughed and said, "We're not kissing cousins, if that's what you're asking!"

The Assistant DA then asked, "What do your parolees call you?" I stated that my parolees address me as either, "Mr. DeWitt, or Officer DeWitt."

I really had a problem with that line of questioning, since most parole agents allowed their parolees to call them by their first name.

Not an hour had past since the Assistant DA left my office when I received a telephone call that went something like this: "Hey, Lonnie!" I then quickly asked, "Who is this?" The voice on the other end then identified himself as the Assistant DA. He really didn't want anything. He simply wanted to see if I would answer to, "Lonnie."

I mentioned this incident to *CJ*, who merely shrugged it off as, "the way they [the DA] do business." After that incident, I allowed all of my parolees to address me as, "Lonnie" if they so desired.

Local law enforcement must get a **big** feather in its cap when it apprehends a bank robber. In fact, that feather must be **so big** that it really doesn't matter whether or not the *right* person is apprehended - just as long as someone - *anyone* - is apprehended and punished.

Two San Jose Police detectives showed me a picture of a Black man robbing a bank. They claimed that the photograph was that of my parolee, Chapman.

To me, the image on the photograph was not very clear and I certainly could not positively identify Chapman as the bank robber. Besides, Chapman was not known to carry a weapon and rob banks. He *hit* small establishments; and a gun was never seen/used. Of course, it was certainly possible for him to have *graduated* into robbing banks.

Again, professional courtesy obligated us (Paroles) to cooperate and arrest Chapman. During my own independent investigation (that Parole Agents are lawfully mandated to undertake), I learned that on the date of the bank robbery, Chapman was at an office party (witnessed by at least two dozen people).

San Jose Police took exception to my investigation and complained to me. At that time, I advised them that I was obligated (as the agent of record) to conduct my own independent investigation.

They, obviously, did not like my response, so they then complained to *CJ* stating that I was, "interfering with their investigation."

The investigators were attempting to fit a square peg into a round hole. They simply had the wrong man arrested; yet, they refused to admit it. While I am not a detective, I do have common sense; and sometimes, I even know how to use it.

I am certain that *CJ* elevated the detectives' complaint. Although *CJ* did not share his concerns (as he seldom did), he made it a point to attend Chapman's Morrissey Hearing (an administrative hearing that determines whether or not a parolee receives an added violation and returns to prison). It was not *normal* for *CJ* to attend these kinds of hearings, as he had *not* done so previously with either any other parole agent or me.

I had the feeling that *CJ* felt that through his presence, I would be less likely to speak on Chapman's behalf. *CJ* obviously underestimated me.

I asked the bank teller, who was present during the hearing, several questions. It became clear to me that the detectives had manipulated the teller's descriptive statement of the bank robber. The teller even testified that Chapman was **not** the robber.

Based on the evidence that I had previously obtained and documented in my written report to the hearing officer (that clearly vindicated Chapman) and the bank teller's own testimony, I asked the hearing officer to immediately release Chapman from local custody.

CJ then interrupted me while I was addressing the hearing officer, stating that my, "opinion" was inappropriate. The hearing officer then interrupted *CJ* and mildly rebuked him by stating, "This is my hearing and Officer DeWitt is encouraged to speak and offer his opinion, as the Agent of Record." With that said, I completed my statements.

The hearing officer agreed with me and the facts presented. Chapman was immediately released from local custody.

CJ attempted to *justify* his comments as we drove back to the parole office; however, I honestly do not know what he said. I had completely tuned *CJ* out.

That was simply just another example reflecting the lack of support that I had learned to expect from *CJ*; and his lack of professional confidence in me. It was also quite obvious to me that *CJ* was embarrassed. I also knew that he had to *report* the outcome of the hearing - *up the chain* - to his supervisors.

Although justice was served, I knew that my position - albeit objective - would not be well received by CDC management.

It soon became apparent to me that the California Department of Corrections had systematically (and conveniently) **imposed a moratorium on both justice and integrity**.

I did receive many thank *you's* from the Chapman family. At that time, I told Chapman, "I want you to know that just as aggressively that I worked toward helping to vindicate you, I would have worked equally as hard to place your ass behind bars, had the facts shown that you were guilty!"

With my assistance, Chapman was arrested by Mountain View Police for drug trafficking a few months later.

While incarcerated, Chapman told me that (although I had him arrested) he, "respected" me for doing my job. He even *apologized* for his letting me down.

Chapter Eleven

Forbidden Friendship

In the late summer of 1992, I met Cathy Brewer while at a supermarket in San Jose. I still smile when I recall the first time I saw Cathy. She drove up and parked next to the curb in front of the supermarket while I was using the telephone. It seemed that every two minutes a child would exit her Volkswagen and go inside the store. That reminded me of the 60's fad when people would literally be stuffed inside a VW just to see how many it would hold. I must have counted a *dozen* children exit that car. Actually, as I later learned, Cathy *only* had five children (all boys). It just *seemed* like more at the time.

To me, Cathy was a sweetheart. She reminded me so much of my mother: *young, single,* and with *so many children.* Cathy and I immediately became very good friends. She told me that she had been married twice; and that she and her present husband were legally separated. Cathy added that he lived, "out-of-State."

I was very happy with my new *relationship* because it gave me the outlet that I needed to, "get a life" and not spend so much overtime in the office during the weekends that I remained in San Jose.

Cathy also valued my friendship. She would occasionally ask my advise on a myriad of subjects ranging from her children's behavioral problems to my suggestions concerning her continuing educational goals. Cathy was currently enrolled in a legal stenographer course.

Although my wife and Cathy had not yet met, they had talked on the telephone with each other. Ruthie was so comfortable with my platonic relationship with Cathy that she even **allowed** Cathy to baby-sit our daughter, Shaneé, on several occasions. Trust me, when I emphasize **allowed**, because neither my wife nor I would trust just *anyone* to watch our daughter.

Cathy and Shaneé quickly became very close. Both were very excited to bake a cake together. Cathy would always say that Shaneé was the daughter that she had always wanted, but never had.

I, too, enjoyed her children. I would take them to the movies, to the park and other such places. They would even *help* me fix their mother's car (which seemed to always need repairing). I was always stopping to help stranded motorists who experienced vehicle difficulties; therefore, it was certainly within character for me to offer my assistance to Cathy. After all, Cathy was - and remains to this day - a very dear friend.

As a retired military member, I had the privilege of residing at Moffett Naval Air Station, on a space available basis during the weekdays. Of course, I would travel home to Sacramento on the weekends. That arrangement worked out great since it was very inexpensive for me to remain in the local area and not be burdened by a difficult commute. However, when the Reserves (Weekend Warriors) were either in town or when there was any kind of special event, all of the billeting spaces were completely filled.

When that occurred, I would oftentimes either sleep in my car or in the billeting office day room (lounge area). The following morning, I would shower in the gymnasium on Moffett and report for work. Cathy would always get angry at me for doing that. She would remind me that I was always welcome to sleep and/or shower at her place. I did not believe that was appropriate since she had children in the household and I always stressed the importance of *perception* and *respect*.

Sometime in late February 1993, Cathy tearfully informed me that her husband, Bret Brewer (who she had previously told me lived, "out-of-State;" and that they were legally separated), was an inmate in a California State prison who would soon parole.

Cathy went on to tell me that her, "relationship with Bret had been over for sometime;" however, she knew that had she initially told me of Bret's CDC-status when we first met that I would not have continued with our *relationship*. Cathy was correct. She needed a friend and I happened to come into her life at that moment.

Of course, I was totally devastated! I then asked her where Bret would be paroling. Cathy told me that she had hoped that he would be assigned to a parole office in San Mateo County (a nearby County where Bret's mother lived); however, Cathy had recently learned that Bret would be assigned somewhere in San Jose.

Cathy felt that if Bret were assigned in San Mateo County that she could have avoided this (out-of-sight, out-of-mind) revelation to me. Cathy begged my forgiveness for her deceit and the potential problems that she may have caused with my peace officer position. Somehow, I fully understood and truly empathized with Cathy and her dilemma. I forgave her.

I silently wished, however, that Bret would be assigned to the Lewis Road Parole Office. Bret paroled in March 1993, and was assigned to a Parole Agent in Unit 5 (as I later learned).

The following month, Ruthie suffered a cerebral aneurysm and came very close to *Death's Door*.

I wanted, so badly, to inform *CJ* and my Regional Administrator of my acquaintance with the wife of a parolee and of the (harmless) circumstances surrounding that friendship. However, my confidence in *CJ* had deteriorated to an unacceptable level where I simply could not trust his judgment in fairly representing me. At the time, I knew very little of Ron Chow, except for the negative feedback that I had gotten from most parole agents (especially the Blacks).

As time passed, I made a very conscious and deliberate decision **not** to involve management in my own personal dilemma. I reasoned that CDC management would simply view my alleged involvement as either a ploy for me to get reassigned to Sacramento (which I had requested following my wife's medical emergency) or, I would be unfairly judged, criticized and ridiculed by management and my peers. I truly believed that my hardship transfer would soon be effective and that I could then put this entire (unfortunate) incident behind me.

Obviously, life is not that simple. In early September 1993, I was under investigation for, "dating" the wife of a parolee. *CJ* was flashing my photograph around Cathy's neighborhood like I was Public Enemy Number One.

In mid-December 1993, I received Notice, "Advisory of Intent to Conduct an Investigatory Interview." Adverse Action was subsequently taken against me for violating California Administrative Code, Title 15, Section 3400 - "Familiarity" and 3406 - "Relatives." I was to receive a one-step salary reduction for 12 months.

On April 4, 1994, I attended a Skelly Hearing. At that time, I submitted the following response to the Deputy Regional Director regarding the above:

Dear Ms. Sager:

On 12-14-93, I received Notice, "Advisory of Intent to Conduct an Investigatory Interview." The letter stated, "Allegations of undue familiarity have been made. This interview will concern your possible violation of California Administrative Code, Director's Title 15, Section 3400 (undue familiarity)."

However, on 3-31-94, I was served with a Notice of Adverse Action citing Section 19574 of the Government Code and Section 3406 (the former of which I am totally unfamiliar).

While the appearance of the proliferation of charges may be cause for future legal discussion still, I will address each allegation mentioned in my Notice of Adverse Action.

iN tHE cAR

STATEMENT OF FACTS

As written: *"On one occasion you assisted his (Bret's) agent, Agent Sherman, in arresting him in her office. Under the circumstances, it could be argued that you would have an ulterior motive in seeing him placed in custody."*

Discussion: *In my opinion, the comments in the second sentence are not "Facts;" therefore, have no place in that portion of the report. Furthermore, I could effectively argue that my refusal to assist another agent in effecting a safe arrest of any parolee would certainly be just cause for my dismissal. Incidentally, I was neither a party to nor had any "input" in staffing parolee Brewer's arrest; therefore, the comments regarding my (possibly) having an ulterior motive are certainly without merit.*

As written: *"By entering into a covert relationship with a parolee's wife, you engaged in undue familiarity."*

Discussion: *My relationship with Cathy was all but, "covert." As previously stated during my investigative interview, Cathy, her children and I spent considerable time together (openly).*

We even had lunch several times at a Burger King in very close proximity to the parole office! Admittedly, however, when she advised me of her husband's CDC-status, our "relationship" was severed (with the exception of isolated conversations) - very public and brief contact.

As written: *"You were dishonest in hiding this information from your employer."*

Discussion: *I take personal and professional exception to the word "dishonest." If, as the "Statement of Facts" imply, I were dishonest and took great pains to enter into a, "covert" relationship with Cathy, why didn't I simply lie and state that I was unaware that Cathy was* married to a parolee? I invite your attention to the "Conclusion" of the Investigating Officer's report: "Without Agent DeWitt's cooperation it would not have been possible to prove a violation had occurred based on information available." That comment certainly does not make me a, "dishonest" person!

Further, a closer look at Director's Rule 3406 does not require the report of "any close friendships with family members of parolees;" rather, it requires the reporting of, "any relative or close friend (of the employee) who has been committed to or transferred to the jurisdiction of the department."

Interestingly, however, Director's Rule 3400 (my "initial" violation charge) states, "....whenever there is reason for an employee to have personal contact or discussions with an inmate or parolee or the family and friends of inmates and parolees, the employee must maintain a helpful but professional attitude and demeanor..." I do believe that I met those requirements.

Ms. Sager, I am not, by any stretch of one's imagination, attempting to absolve myself from any wrongdoing. In fact, on the contrary! I still admit culpability in (1) continuing to communicate with Cathy (upon knowing of her husband's status); and (2) failing to notify my supervisor(s) of my acquaintance with Cathy.

I fully recognize management's inherent responsibility in ensuring standards of conduct are consistently maintained by all employees. Further, when an employee falls short of expected standards, swift and fair punishment is expected by all (including the offender) to help maintain the highest levels of discipline. Ms. Sager, while I do expect to be "punished" for my breach in discipline, I ask that you consider that (1) throughout the entire investigative process, I have not only been cooperative but extremely candid in my statements; (2) that my, "relationship" with Cathy was that of a, "good friend" and I had no ulterior motives; and, (3) that I remained objective throughout my conversations with her. I even asked her to "be patient and supportive" of her husband.

In addition, Ms. Sager, as you well know, an Adverse Action in my personnel file is equivalent to an "R" suffix [that identifies "Rapists" *and other sexual predators] in a convict's "jacket" - the kiss of death (as it relates to special assignments, promotions, etc.,)! I really don't believe that I deserve that.*

Lastly, any decrease in my pay would financially devastate me. As you are aware, I am trying to maintain two "residences;" and I am barely keeping afloat.

Ms. Sager, please consider the merits of my comments during your discretionary review.

Sincerely, Lonnie F. DeWitt

During my Skelly Hearing Ms. Sager asked me, "What action can I take to make you happy?" I replied, "You can either give me a verbal warning or a Letter of Instruction." I must have given the wrong answer. On April 6, 1994, Ms. Sager modified my Notice of Adverse Action and amended the final action to "a one step pay reduction for six months."

This quote from *CJ* bears repeating:

"Without Agent DeWitt's cooperation it would not have been possible to prove a violation had occurred based on information available."

That statement was an extremely rare moment of "objectivity" in *CJ's* life. I later thanked him for his objective reporting.

I can certainly appreciate the necessity of rules addressing "unfamiliarity;" still, I have difficulty with the legality of that Director's Rule since it places unequal restrictions (that result in unequal administrative reporting requirements) to a select group of people - Black correctional staff. Approximately one-third of California's prison populace is comprised of Black Americans. That, in itself, should be alarming; especially, when we consider that Black Americans reflect only 10% of California's population.

Let's now consider the massive numbers of Black parolees. It does not take a rocket scientist to figure out that simply given the totality of

Black inmates and parolees (and the small numbers that Blacks reflect in California's overall population) - a great majority of Black correctional staff have a family member or a personal friend either incarcerated in our State penal institutions, or on parole. The DeWitt family is no exception.

In America, a White family can travel from East to West (coast to coast) and **not** make contact with anyone who would fit into the Director's (familiarity) Rules. A Black family, on the other hand, cannot walk from their residence to the corner store without making *at least one* such contact!

To avoid this dilemma, many Black correctional staff simply avoid contact with other Blacks who are non-peace officers. The Director's Rule is, therefore, a racist set-up. It's one of those **I gotcha** for the unsuspecting Black staff who fails to report an off-duty *contact* (with a parolee, a friend or a family member of either a parolee or an inmate) to *Big Daddy*. Even though other law enforcement agencies are generally the ones who routinely make the *initial* arrest, they have no such (*familiarity*) restrictions. That *Director's Rule* is clearly unrealistic, unacceptable and lends itself to *selective enforcement.*

Most of my Black brothers and my Black sisters live *across the tracks*. Therefore, some (Black peace officers) oftentimes cringe when they meet new faces for fear of their having relatives within the CDC System. That *meeting* would, of course, necessitate *mandatory* documenting and subsequent reporting requirements.

At one point following his investigation, *CJ* looked at me and asked, "Couldn't you tell by the way the apartment looked that her husband was on parole?" That dumb, stereo-typical question was certainly *within character* of that (anal retentive) supervisor. One day, he'll *awaken* to discover that *some* parolees and their families live better than he ever will.

While I was working OD (Officer of the Day) duties, Bret telephoned me. He apologized for the problems that he had caused me, stating that he had found out the, "truth" (about my *relationship*) after talking with Cathy, their relatives, and some of her friends. At that time, I told Bret that I forgave him but the, "damage" had already been done. I thanked him for being, "man enough" to apologize. At that moment, Bret showed more compassion, concern, and empathy for my feelings than all of California Department of Corrections management combined. For that, I thank him.

Bret is now back at home (prison). I understand that he received eight to eleven years, this time.

Cathy and Bret divorced shortly after Bret's initial parole.

Cathy would later meet and marry Kenslo, an extraordinary man. This is not our son, Kenslo; however, Ruthie and I would have been thrilled and honored to have Cathy as a daughter-in-law.

Ruthie, Shaneé and I witnessed Kenslo and Cathy exchange their holy vows of matrimony, during a beautiful wedding ceremony held at their home in San Jose, California.

Kenslo and Cathy are the proud parents of a beautiful baby girl, Kuliya Shukriya, born June 8, 1995. In Greek, **Shukriya** means, **"Thankful."** Cathy finally has the daughter she had always wanted. Kenslo, Cathy and Kuliya Shukriya are all, most assuredly, **"thankful."**

Alice Lee Combs (DeWitt)

Ruthie Louise DeWitt

"The Reunion"
(Pictured from left to right): Johnny Ray Combs, Jr., Deborah Lynn Combs (Guillory), Carol Ann DeWitt (Borges), Lonnie Faustino DeWitt, John DeWitt and James Edward DeWitt

Kenslo Gary DeWitt   Lonnie Faustino DeWitt, Jr.

Shaneé Faustina DeWitt

Chapter Twelve

Ruthie

uthie, my loving companion. My wife and friend for nearly three decades.

I cannot possibly conclude this book without mentioning my wife. Although most of our friends call her Ruthie, her family and I have always called her *Louise* - Ruthie's middle name. Since *Louise* sounds a little *too Country*, I'll use Ruthie.

Without Ruthie, my life would be empty - incomplete. I thank God for allowing our love to flourish from our early childhood days of the 1960s into our adulthood.

Ruthie has truly been my Guardian Angel throughout my entire adult life. Ruthie has been my Rock.

On our 25th wedding anniversary, April 13, 1993, Ruthie suffered a cerebral aneurysm and was immediately hospitalized. Within a week of that medical crisis, I applied for a *hardship* transfer to either a parole office in Sacramento or the parole office in Stockton (a distance of only 35 miles from our home).

My personal concerns for Ruthie's welfare were visibly evident throughout my repeated communications with CDC officials. Unfortunately, these officials failed (by default) to either fully recognize or appreciate my inherent responsibilities as a concerned husband; as a loving father; as a man. That, was the thrust of my greatest heartburn.

My love and devotion to my family provided the stimulus for me to continue with my efforts to effect my reassignment to the Sacramento/Stockton area. Even though I soon realized that my exertions were exercises in futility; still, I owed it to Ruthie and my daughter to try.

I prayed to God for **Him** to spare Ruthie's life as she lay in bed (near death) in intensive care following her cerebral aneurysm. I thank God that **He** allowed her to continue in this life with me.

When Shaneé telephoned and hysterically told me, "Mom is in the hospital!" My heart seemed to stop beating! I had so many questions that I dared not ask my ten year-old daughter! In fact, some of the questions that I had, I really didn't want to hear the answers: "How much pain had Ruthie endured?" "Would Shaneé be motherless?" "Would I soon become a widower?"

After informing *CJ* of my wife's hospitalization, I immediately drove to Kaiser Hospital in North Sacramento (where she had been transported, by ambulance, from South Kaiser). By the time I arrived, Ruthie's many cousins, aunts and friends - who lived locally - were already there, standing vigil by her bedside.

iN tHE cAR

When I looked into my wife's eyes, I thought that I saw the face of a dying person - *Ruthie* - who *still showed character.*

I stood there, *physically well*; yet, I lacked the strength that my *dying* wife possessed. Of course, at the time, I didn't realize it but I was the one who was really (spiritually) sick and dying.

When I saw Ruthie *hooked* to a heart monitor and other medical gadgets, I really went into total shock! Ruthie and I laugh about it now; but, I looked at her and asked two questions: "How are you feeling, Louise?" And almost in the same breath, I asked, "Did you mail off our income taxes?" How stupid and insensitive could I be? How could I even begin to think about, "income taxes" while my wife was in acute pain and near death? The only plausible explanation that I have to offer is that I went into total shock and simply could not think of anything else to say. Still, how insensitive!

Looking back at that, sort of reminds me of some White people who, while at a loss for words, will ask a Black person, "You been staying outta trouble?" Or, they will say, "You stay outta trouble, now!" Oh, yes, let's not forget about the real insensitive comment, *"....you people."*

Maybe, we're all victims of total **inshockentivity!**

I really couldn't believe that I asked my *dying* wife that question. God forgive me. When I arrived home, I began to tremble as the reality of losing my loving companion seemed imminent. I wept and begged God to spare Ruthie's life and to forgive me for my **inshockentivity!**

I felt so helpless and powerless. I simply could not handle it. I decided to return to work and let others *deal* with that cerebral aneurysm thing.

While in the hospital, Ruthie had a mysterious female visitor (that she did not recognize and cannot recognize, to this day). That woman placed her hands on Ruthie's feet and said, **"Pray with me."** My wife does not remember if she and the woman prayed silently or aloud; however, Ruthie very distinctively recalls that she could feel the heat (all over her body) from the woman's hands when that mysterious woman touched her feet.

The woman then said, **"Don't worry, you're not going to have** surgery tomorrow. **God will take care of you!"**

Ruthie's surgery was scheduled for the following morning.

That morning, the doctor told Ruthie that the surgical team wanted to do an angiogram before surgery to, "see exactly what we're dealing with." Following the angiogram, the doctor then said, "You're a lucky young woman. When we did the angiogram, we saw that the leak was beginning to seal itself, so we catheterized and sealed it off. There's no guarantee it will work; it could blow anytime."

Those doctors may choose to believe whatever they wish; however, they were dealing with God where *luck* was not part of the equation and God guarantees **His** product.

Ruthie's *miracle recovery* didn't come with a 3-year, 50,000 mile warranty. There was no tag or label showing that her recovery was, "Made in Korea," "Made in Japan," or even, "Made in America." Ruthie has an eternal warranty that reads, "Made in God" with a lifetime-plus guarantee!

My wife has not been hospitalized since that incident, over four years ago. **God lookin' out!**

Not one person within the entire California Department of Corrections even bothered to telephone Ruthie and see how she was doing. There were no cards; no letters. Even my immediate supervisor, *CJ* - following CDC's fine tradition - showed zero compassion and concern for the DeWitt family.

It seemed that I was given an (undocumented) ultimatum by the California Department of Corrections - suggesting that I decide on either my job or my family.

Well, there was really no contest. My family *won*. Even as I face bankruptcy, I am proud of the actions that I took to effect my transfer. I am, however, not proud of the actions (or the lack thereof) taken by that infamous *Dynamic Trio*.

I'll eventually get another job. But, I'll always have Ruthie (even in death - hers or mine) in my heart.

Having been a senior military manager, it was difficult for me to comprehend the minuscule value that CDC placed on the welfare of its minority workforce and their families.

While totally ignoring CDC's not-so-subtle opposition, I began my efforts to effect an emergency hardship transfer to be with my family. My job, at that point, was to provide emotional support to Ruthie and help stabilize the DeWitt household.

Whenever the good Lord finds it within **His** mercy to call me home, I don't want Ruthie to weep. Instead, I want her to simply remember the wonderful times that we shared and the beautiful children that God blessed us to watch for **Him**.

As I continue my daily emotional struggles in this healing process, Ruthie remains the one *constant force* in my life.

Regardless of life's difficulties, I will continue to treat my *African Queen* like a queen. As the *Mother of the Earth*, she deserves no less. Ruthie is the *Queen of the Nile*; she stands vigilant, my *Amazon Soldier*.

Ruthie, my *loving companion*, my *lovely wife*, my *true friend*, my *childhood sweetheart*, my *Guardian Angel*, my *Rock*, my *African Queen*, my *Amazon Soldier*, continues to guide me as I valiantly march, in precise military cadence, beyond the pain.

Chapter Thirteen

Against My Objections

y professional confidence in *CJ* had all but deteriorated over the past several months because it became evident that he intentionally failed to either tutor, mentor, or provide any support to Black parole agents.

CJ even gave me the appearance that he viewed my wife's medical emergency as a non-emergency and that his primary concerns were principally focused on *mission accomplishment and **nothing** else.*

My urgent letter requesting a hardship transfer to Ronald Chow, Regional II Administrator, read:

♦♦♦

Dear Mr. Chow:

Regrettably, I must request consideration for an immediate hardship/humanitarian reassignment to Region I (Sacramento/Stockton area).

On April 13, 1993, (my 25th wedding anniversary), my wife suffered an aneurysm that required her immediate intensive care hospitalization. She remained in the Intensive Care Unit following a series of extensive medical examinations, which included a cerebral angiogram, CT, MRI and spinal tap. Fortunately, the vein that burst (which would normally have resulted in cerebral hemorrhaging), "sealed" itself; thereby, eliminating the need for immediate surgery and reducing/delaying chronic medical problems known to cause permanent paralysis.

As a responsible and responsive husband, it's critical that I am reasonably available to meet my wife's medical and psychological needs. Mr. Chow, as a manager, I fully realize that you have many management concerns to consider.

Therefore, let me share with you some of the relocation efforts that I made and ongoing sacrifices taken, when you initially hired me, over a year ago (for which I am truly grateful).

* My wife and I had our home appraised. Unfortunately, however, because of the economic downturn, we stood to lose between $15,000 - $20,000 had we sold our home.

* We home "shopped" in the San Jose area and, although San Jose was also experiencing an economic down-turn, we discovered that a comparable (2,600 sq. ft, 5-bedroom, 3-bath, 3-car garage) home, with a swimming pool, in the San Jose area would cost me your salary!

* The unreasonably high cost of housing in the San Jose area coupled with the substantial loss in selling our home were the primary reasons that my wife and I elected to keep our home in Sacramento.

iN tHE cAR

Recurring issues, regarding my job security as a Parole Agent, basically solidified our decision not to sell.

* I briefly resided with my relatives in San Jose; and, *I stress briefly, because of incompatible lifestyles.*

* *For the most part, however, I reside in the Bachelor Enlisted Quarters on Moffett Naval Air Station (to which I am entitled as a retired military member), during the weekdays and, "commute" home (260 miles round-trip) on the weekends.*

Mr. Chow, I realize that it was my decision to accept employment in San Jose and, it was essentially my decision not to relocate my family to the San Jose area (not withstanding my financial devastation that would have resulted).

Still, I respectfully ask that you consider the merits of my request (given my wife's present medical condition); and, the proactive ("good faith") efforts that I have either taken or am currently taking to help ensure a positive balance (given the present circumstances) between work and home. Also, please understand, that I am simply providing you with specifics to assist you in your decision; this is not a complaint, as I am neither a complainer nor a whiner.

Mr. Chow, I am very disciplined so, please rest assured that I will accept your decision regardless of the outcome. Whether I remain in Region II or, if I am transferred to Region I (at no expense to the Department), I intend to remain a loyal and dedicated employee.

Sincerely, Lonnie F. DeWitt

Like most personnel issues, within the California Department of Corrections, mine became a guessing game. I really did not know who recommended what, since Ron Chow had not provided me with a written response to my request.

During the next **seventeen months** of attempting to effect this hardship transfer, I fully documented and prepared a Chronology of Events to show all the good faith actions that I was taking to help expedite my already overdue hardship transfer to Sacramento.

It soon became bitterly clear to me that CDC management simply did not care.

At the onset of my attempts to effect this transfer, *CJ* had the occasion to tell me, "**Against my objections**, Ron Chow will probably approve your transfer!" *CJ* went on to say that his, *"position"* was strictly a, *"management decision"* and that it had nothing to do with me. He further stated that if he lost me that the other parole agents would have to absorb my caseload. The reality was that if I were transferred, *CJ* would then have to absorb the increased workload with his other agents; however, **if I were terminated, he would be authorized my replacement.**

Bull's-eye! *CJ's* insensitivity finally struck a nerve. That conversation will forever haunt me. Not because of *CJ's* comments; because, by then, I expected no less from him. But, several months earlier, *CJ did not hesitate* to transfer a (non-Black) parole agent, who was not experiencing a hardship, to be closer to home.

Upon that agent's departure, the other parole agents and I quickly absorbed his caseload, without complaint or controversy.

Although *CJ* said that, "Ron Chow will probably approve your transfer" still, I saw nothing in writing from Ron Chow either supporting or denying my relocation efforts.

I spoke with Mr. Henry Portolla, Region I Administrator (the person who had primary responsibility in either accepting or denying my transfer request into *his* Region) and followed up on that telephone conversation in my September 7, 1993, letter to him:

Dear Mr. Portolla:

Several months ago, you and I spoke concerning my request for an EOT reassignment to the Sacramento/Stockton area based on a bonafide medical hardship. At that time, however, transfers between regions were not considered (pending a decision involving other parole agents who were transferred).

I understand that management and union officials have reached an agreement; therefore, I am resubmitting my EOT application for your favorable consideration.

Please find enclosed a copy of my April 20, 1993, letter to my Regional Administrator, Mr. Chow, who recommended approval of my initial transfer request.

Sincerely, Lonnie F. DeWitt

Mr. Portolla responded in his October 6, 1993, letter to me:

Dear Mr. DeWitt:

This memorandum is in response to your Employee Opportunity Transfer (E.O.T.) request.

Your name will be placed on the E.O.T. list; however, I must advise you that the Re-employment list has precedence at this time. The E.O.T. list will not be utilized until the Re-employment list has been exhausted. I do not anticipate that this will occur in the near future.

Your E.O.T. request did not include a completed State application. An application is needed in order to calculate your placement on the list. Please forward it to the attention of Kelly Madlinger, Staff Services Analyst, Region I, Parole and Community Services Division.

Your transfer request will be kept on file at Region I Headquarters as openings occur in the future, your E.O.T. will be reviewed by the Parole Administrators and Unit Supervisors in your areas of interest.

Sincerely, Henry A. Portolla

By now, I had the feeling that I was being jerked around by that cruel, unjust, and shamelessly callous System we call the California Department of Corrections. Upon receipt of Mr. Portolla's letter, I immediately sent him the following response, dated November 11, 1993, and followed-up with a personal visit to his office within a week following this letter:

◆ ◆ ◆

Dear Mr. Portolla:

I must, once again, appeal to you as a humane and professional manager to consider my personal family hardship and take appropriate action to help me alleviate some of my frustrations by permitting me to join your team in the Sacramento/Stockton area as a Parole Agent 1, field agent.

While you are already aware of the medical crisis that my wife suffered in April of this year, please allow me to share some of my concerns and frustrations.

In the event of an immediate medical emergency, I believe that it's not only critical, but also important, that I be reasonably available to meet my wife's medical and psychological needs.

Last night, while traveling from San Jose to Sacramento (a trip that normally takes two and a half-hours), I was "stuck" in traffic because of a vehicular accident. That trip took exactly five hours to complete! Fortunately, I was traveling in a non-emergency situation. And, as you are aware, as we enter into the winter season, driving conditions worsen.

Mr. Portolla, notwithstanding my wife's medical problems, as a parent, it is imperative that I maintain adequate parental stability in my household for my 10-year old daughter - please give me that opportunity.

Sincerely, Lonnie F. DeWitt

◆ ◆ ◆

My face-to-face meeting with Portolla did nothing to persuade him. He did, however, comment on my using the word, *"humane"* in my letter. At the time, I had no clue to what Portolla alluded. However, in time, I would learn that the letters **"h-u-m-a-n-e"** had no place in CDC correspondence. I quickly learned that **CDC was the antonym of humane**.

As you may have guessed, by now, Mr. Portolla and I became

virtual pen pals. I use the word *pal* very loosely, however. Mr. Portolla's written response to me, dated November 18, 1993:

♦ ♦ ♦

Lonnie F. DeWitt
(Note: No More "Dear Mr. DeWitt")
This is in response to your recent letter regarding your transfer request.
Please understand that it is not within my purview to grant your request. As you were told previously, the Department's agreement with CCPOA requires us to exhaust the reemployment list before using any other means to fill positions.
We therefore, cannot approve transfers for any reason. I recommend that if you have not already done so, you contact the two Folsom institutions as well as Mule Creek, Deuel Vocational Institution and Northern California Women's Facility and apply for a Correctional Counselor I position. A position in one of those institutions may be of benefit to you and your family.
Good Luck, Henry A. Portolla

♦ ♦ ♦

By now, I was somewhat annoyed and angered by the negative responses from CDC officials. All I was hearing was how I could not be helped, rather than how my transfer could be effected where I could remain a parole agent. First of all, it's important to understand that while this entire letter writing was going on, **other** parole agents were being transferred throughout the State of California.

Secondly, it is common knowledge throughout the State of California that CDC management does whatever it wants; to whomever it wants; and whenever it wants.

I am, therefore, convinced that although I had a valid emergency hardship, someone (in management) was determined not to effect my transfer - even, at the risk of *lying* - which is *exactly* what happened.

During one of my weekdays off, I took the time to personally hand-deliver the following letter, dated March 10, 1994, to the Deputy Director, Parole and Community Services Division, Marsha Morales:

◆◆◆

Dear Ms. Morales:

I am requesting your personal intervention and assistance in helping my reassignment efforts from the San Jose area to the Sacramento/Stockton areas as a Parole Agent-1 (my current position). The attached documents clearly reflect that my request is based on a bonafide medical hardship.

Please note that my hardship reassignment request - which, if approved, would be at no expense to the State - has been in the "system" nearly one year without (positive) results!

While I will not comment on management's position to arbitrarily and unilaterally deny all intra-Regional transfer requests by Parole Agents until our present redeployment list is exhausted - a process that may take five years - I will, however, unequivocally state that this decision has caused unnecessary "casualties" among Parole Agents and their families; and, has further widened the gap of distrust and discontent between rank-and-file and management.

I recently read Director Gonzalez's article in the Correction News, "Treatment of People - the Theme for the Future," with much pride and enthusiasm. For most of us, however, the Future is Now!

Ms. Morales, thank you very much for taking the time (out of your very busy and hectic schedule) to read this letter. I do hope that my candid comments did not, in any way, detract from my overall desired intentions (of having you in "my corner" to assist me). Ms. Morales, I do need your help in this matter.

Sincerely, Lonnie F. DeWitt

◆◆◆

Now, anyone in his (or her) *right mind* would have known that my letter would not generate a positive reception. Well, it apparently didn't. In fact, **Her Highness** elected to disregard and not even *bother* to answer my letter.

Over one year had past since my wife's medical emergency; and still, no results. I then sent the following letter, dated April 26, 1994, to Mr. Chow:

◆ ◆ ◆

Dear Mr. Chow:

I must, once again, solicit your personal support in helping my reassignment efforts to the Sacramento/Stockton area. As you are aware, my initial reassignment efforts (over a year ago), were essentially based on my wife's very serious medical condition.

I must now inform you that my immediate reassignment is crucial to my financial solvency, the mental health of my family and, to my own mental and physical health. I've satisfactorily completed my two-year Apprenticeship Program while in San Jose and, by all accounts, my job performance remains at or above established standards. I've performed my duties under the most austere conditions - having to commute home on the weekends for nearly two years!

Lately, however, I have had to commute home daily (a distance of 260 miles round-trip) to attend to the psychological needs of my 10-year old daughter (see enclosed Sacramento Police Department Report). My daughter is still suffering emotionally from her traumatic experience and, as long as my health lasts, I will continue my commute, if necessary.

Although I do have relatives in San Jose, I have no stable residence; and now that Moffett Naval Air Station (my previous semi-permanent residence) has closed, my out-of-pocket expenses have increased four times my average weekly expenditures! The one night (4-19-94) that my health would not allow my commute home, I remained overnight in a downtown San Jose Inn, which cost me $48.40 (copy of receipt enclosed).

Mr. Chow, I simply cannot afford to remain overnight in San Jose for any length of time! I really do need your help, Mr. Chow; and I need it now!   Sincerely, Lonnie F. DeWitt

◆ ◆ ◆

My enclosure included the Sacramento Police Department Report of a *Suspicious Person* who, while driving his vehicle, made several U-turns and appeared to follow my daughter, Shaneé, as she walked home from school. This incident really disturbed my daughter, which caused her to have recurring nightmares for quite some time.

Ironically, this incident occurred exactly one year from the date that my wife suffered her cerebral aneurysm. I was not even aware of this coincidence until I began writing my book.

Chow answered my letter. Unfortunately, his May 2, 1994, letter to me was more of a *reprimand than one of assistance*, as I had previously (and on several occasions) requested:

Mr. DeWitt, I received your letter of April 26, 1994. I am sorry to hear about your family situation and sincerely hope that both your wife and daughter's conditions are improving.

I must again remind you that your request to transfer must be processed to Region I, rather than to Region II, as I do not have the authority to process nor approve it.

Also, your letter indicates that you are no longer complying with the conditions of your employment to reside within thirty-five miles of your assignment. I must remind you that failure to maintain this requirement can result in your termination under the provisions of Government Code Section 19585. Based upon the family situation identified in your memo, I will approve a maximum sixty-day temporary exception to this condition of employment for you to address your residence situation. At the end of the sixty days, you must provide your supervisor with a local residence within thirty-five miles at which you can be reached. You shall park the state car at the office daily for overnight storage during this sixty-day period.

You were advised of this requirement at the time of hire, and it is your responsibility to comply. You should have also advised your supervisor in advance of your decision to commute back and forth to the Sacramento area and of your inability to comply with the employment condition.

You may wish to consider a transfer to a CDC institution as a resolution to your situation.

You are to advise your supervisor of your local residence address compliance or other intentions on or before June 30, 1994. Failure to do so can result in your separation.

Signed: Ronald Chow

◆ ◆ ◆

I must really be naïve. For some unknown reason, I truly expected some empathy from my Regional Administrator. Instead, I heard, "I am sorry....." Well, *"sorry" is a sorry (ass) word!* Chow could have kept his, *"sorry"* words to himself.

Departmental managers were constantly advising me that they could not effect my transfer because of our California Correctional Peace Officers Association (CCPOA) Union; however, my Union representative was telling me that CDC *could* and *should* effect my transfer.

My Union Representative, Mark Vinch, advised me that Henry Portolla told him that the reason why I was not being considered for a transfer was because, **"You knew about your wife's medical condition *prior* to accepting your assignment to San Jose."** That is beyond ludicrousness!

If anyone has ever (or knows someone who has ever) experienced a cerebral aneurysm, it is unmistakably clear that an aneurysm is likened to a light bulb - when it blows, it blows! There simply isn't any warning.

For Portolla to make the statement that I knew about my wife's medical condition *prior* to accepting my San Jose assignment (a year earlier), is **dumber than dumb!**

Portolla's extensive knowledge of the medical field is about as useless as a teaspoon of water poured on a forest fire; and not nearly as effective.

In an obvious attempt to either validate or justify its callous indifference, that same CDC *clown*, Portolla, told me of another parole agent whose request for transfer was also denied by the Department even though that agent's wife was hospitalized (in a coma) and they had three school age children. Has the California Department of Corrections gone raving mad, or what?

I would really like to know exactly *what* died and left those brainless, heartless Kreatures in charge!

I then contacted Angelo Figueroa, a well respected San Jose Mercury News Staff Reporter, and asked him to intervene on my behalf by contacting Portolla.

Shortly thereafter, I *heard it through the grapevine* that Portolla told his staff, **"DeWitt is off-limits to Region 1!"**

My *helpful* Union, the California Correctional Peace Officers Association (CCPOA), (aka: California Correctional Peckerwood Officers Association), *failed* to even utter one word of disapproval or protest against the California Department of Corrections for the injustice and obvious unequal treatment that I, a Black peace officer, was being subjected.

CCPOA, one of the largest and most powerful union in the State of California - that has even taken the California State Personnel Board to court on issues affecting White correctional staff – looked the other way while I was being *whiteballed*. It became apparent to me that I was paying monthly dues into a *color-struck account*.

In fact, my Union Representative, Mark Vinch, became conveniently unavailable to further discuss my hardship transfer issues.

On May 18, 1994, I wrote the following letter to my Assemblyman, Philip Isenberg, followed by yet another personal visit to CDC Central Office in downtown Sacramento (appealing for assistance):

◆ ◆ ◆

Dear Phil:

I am a State Parole Agent assigned to San Jose, Unit #5. On April 13, 1993, my wife suffered an aneurysm that required her immediate hospitalization in the intensive care unit. On April 20, 1993,

(Enclosure 1), I submitted a request for an immediate hardship/humanitarian reassignment to Region 1 (Sacramento/Stockton area).

Now, a year later, followed by several letters of requests and one face-to-face meeting with Mr. Portolla (Regional 1 Administrator and sole approving/disapproving authority), my efforts have failed to achieve the desired objective of my attending to the psychological needs of my family while adding to the stability of the DeWitt family.

On March 10, 1994, (Enclosure 6), I wrote Ms. Morales, Deputy Director of Corrections, a letter requesting her personal intervention and assistance in helping me with my request for transfer; and I personally hand carried the letter to her office.

To date, my March 10, 1994 letter to her remains unanswered! Incidentally, the only "word" that I received after writing my letter to Ms. Morales, was part of "rumor control" (through the grapevine) that, "DeWitt is off-limits to Region 1!"

On April 26, 1994 (Enclosure 7), I submitted another letter to Mr. Chow, my Regional II Administrator, apprising him of my ten-year old daughter's traumatic experience and the need for my daily presence in the household (as opposed to my weekend presence for the past two years). In the letter, I also explained my current financial difficulties that were caused by my separation from my family and further aggravated by the closure of Moffett Naval Air Station (my temporary "residence").

On May 2, 1994 (Enclosure 8), Mr. Chow responded to my letter.

*I will reiterate (**with emphasis**) what I stated in my letter to Mr. Chow, "....as long as my health lasts, I will continue to commute, if necessary."*

I'm asking for your personal intervention to help expedite my transfer to Sacramento. Mr. Chow has given me until June 30, 1994, to advise my supervisor of my local San Jose residence or face separation.

Phil, as I have fully explained to Mr. Chow, I have no resources in San Jose and I have no intentions of now establishing my residence there. My family is very comfortable in Sacramento!

My request for transfer does not constitute a precedence. Parole Agents from all over California have been routinely transferred to and from Region I for reasons ranging from "nicety" to "convenience" to "hardships."

As a matter-of-record, Region I is in need of Parole Agents; however, since Mr. Portolla enjoys the luxury of "selecting" his own Agents, it appears that I certainly won't be one of them (barring any outside intervention)!

To date, CDC management has shown zero-regard for the DeWitt family and, the 260-mile commute that I face daily! I give parolees on my caseload more consideration; and, I certainly show more concern!

I served my Country honorably for 23 years while in military uniform. I already fought my "war" in Vietnam - is it really necessary that I fight another "war" (with CDC)? Let's hope not, because I am not the enemy!

What does it take to end this appearance of second-class citizenry? It is quite apparent that if management had the best interest of the DeWitt family at heart, I would have long since been transferred to the Sacramento area to join my family rather than my having to play this "commute" and "weekend husband-father game!" I have been totally isolated from my family and community for two years -- Enough, is enough! Hopefully, Phil, you'll care enough to put an end to this tragic exploitation of resource!

Further, I don't need to be given an "ultimatum" by my Regional Administrator with the threat of employment termination unless I establish a residence within the San Jose community (in 60 days). Incidentally, during my two-year commute between San Jose and Sacramento, I have never been late in reporting for work!

Has the Department of Corrections become so callous, complacent, and comfortable in its blatant disregard for its staff that it can afford to openly show its insensitivity on personal issues affecting selected individuals?

Why should I have to seek legislative relief for a simple administrative action that would not cost the State a thin dime?

As a matter of note, during my commute, I have personally arrested (detained) a drunk driver and passenger who created a seriously potential hazard on Interstate 5. I also personally rescued a driver who was forced down a 50-foot embankment and whose car overturned, by pulling him out of the window of the wrecked vehicle. I applied medical first aid (while treating the driver for shock) until the CHP arrived. Again, I personally pulled a truck driver from the cab of his vehicle after a multi-vehicle accident on Interstate 880.

I mention these feats not for personal credit or recognition because, until now, each has gone unnoticed (except possibly by the persons I helped). I wish only to make one statement regarding my actions - I am a professional, total team player and I refuse to be treated any less! I am very comfortable with whom I am; and I don't need to honk my own horn for recognition.

Phil, I truly apologize for my having to ask you for your personal assistance in resolving a matter that should have been resolved long ago within my departmental channels. However, I do ask that you insist that my transfer to Sacramento (as a case-carrying Parole Agent-1) be effective immediately to allow me to add much needed stability to the DeWitt family while minimizing the hazards of my commute.

Sincerely, Lonnie F. DeWitt

Shortly thereafter, I met with a representative from Assemblyman Isenberg's office; however, there was nothing substantial to report. There was some communication between my Assemblyman, CCPOA and Departmental officials.

My letter to Assemblyman Isenberg, of course, embarrassed CDC officials. *First*, I was verbally told that, **"We didn't receive your March 10, 1994 letter."**

Then, after explaining that I personally hand carried and gave the letter to Ms. Morales' secretary, the *second* story was, **"We answered your letter."**

Then, almost out of the same breath, I heard the *third story*, **"We must have misplaced your letter because of our office move."** *Finally*, I was told, **"We apologize. We're preparing a response to your letter now."**

Four months after my initial letter to Ms Morales, **Ms. Thang** sent the following response, dated July 1, 1994:

◆ ◆ ◆

Dear Mr. DeWitt

This is in response to your letter concerning assistance with your Hardship Transfer Request. Please accept our apologies for the lateness in our response.

As you know, last year's budget adversely impacted the Division and we were forced to layoff or transfer many of our parole agents to other classifications. This year the Chief Deputy Director, R.H. Denninger, authorized the Parole and Community Services Division to rehire these parole agents.

Currently, any vacant position for the parole agent classification must be filled with employees who are on the subdivisional and departmental re-employment lists. Those agents on the re-employment lists are contacted for interest for a vacant position in their respective region and then on a statewide basis. We are unable to fill vacant positions until the re-employment lists are exhausted.

When the lists are cleared, we may then utilize other methods of hiring agents such as the employee opportunity transfer method.

We sympathize and understand the urgency of your request. However, at this time, we are unable to assist you. You are encouraged to obtain the job opportunity bulletin that is provided by the Department on current vacancies and pursue other options. I am sending a copy of your application to the Wardens at Folsom State Prison, California State Prison - Sacramento and Mule Creek State Prison for their consideration as vacancies occur. Best wishes for your success in finding suitable employment close to home.

If you have any questions, please feel free to contact Gene Suna, Employee Relations Officer, at (telephone number given).

Sincerely, Marsha Morales

(Signed "4" by Robert A. Ruffate)

    This remotely reminds me of a conversation that I had, with an Air Force major, while in the military. Although I am now uncertain of the subject, I do recall the major replying to me, "I really sympathize with you, Sergeant DeWitt."

My response to that Air Force officer was, "Major, if I wanted 'sympathy' I'm sure that I can find it in Websters [Dictionary] - somewhere between 'shit' and 'syphilis'!" The major and I both fell out laughing. Of course, he and I were the best of friends; and I felt comfortable in being somewhat flippant with him.

Neither Morales nor Ruffate and I enjoy such a relationship; therefore, they can both keep their, "sympathy" to themselves.

Superficially, that letter really sounds legitimate (if you choose to believe CDC's *communicative diarrhea*). The Japanese call that, *"urusai"* (ugly noise). The *real* truth, however, exists between the covers of this book; and it is about to unfold.

Even I know the difference between *piss* and *rain*.

Chapter Fourteen

Buzzards vs. Vultures

I truly hesitate to use the term *buzzard* because even a lowly *buzzard* has the good graces to swoop down on *still* and *lifeless* animals. I would much rather prefer to call *some* of the California Department of Corrections management and staff, *"vultures"* because of their ability to eat their young alive and frequent need to scavenge.

Even the most cowardly supervisor gets bold and openly lavishes on the taste of blood; on the taste of victory in swallowing one of its young and devouring the caucus.

While not necessarily viewed as a Black-White issue, one will invariably see that the devouree is most often a person of Color while the devourer is most often White.

All of these *wannabe devourers* - Black, White, Hispanics, and others - eat out of the same plate of corruption and dine at the same table of ignorance. Some, eventually go on to receive their fiery baptism in hatred.

These little tin pseudo-soldiers, with their shining badges and lethal batons, are general inept when it comes to effective communication (written and oral), adult-to-adult transactional analysis, and good management principles and practices.

These same correctional staff are generally overly aggressive and assertive when it comes to *ratpacking* (when two or more correctional staff *jump* on one inmate). That is common in CDC. Or, when it comes to squeezing the trigger to possibly take someone's life during an altercation (that's almost always between inmates).

Obviously, we do have our exceptions. There is a great number of highly proficient and professional correctional staff who may continually be relied upon to offer an unbiased approach to any given situation. Unfortunately, the great majority are line staff who are seldom asked for either their opinions, feedback or meaningful cross-feed of information.

In my opinion, people who, because of the nature of their employment, carry a weapon should be subject to both psychological examination and frequent (unannounced) drug testing by an independent (non-State) agency.

However, because Department of Corrections takes care of **its own** (who are *iN tHE cAR*), many correctional staff members, who are known to either personally use drugs or who have been caught selling drugs to convicts, are still allowed to remain peace officers.

Conversely, administrative remedies affecting minority correctional staff who become involved in adverse actions are harshly viewed by CDC management. Consequently, more often than not, the combined mentalities of CDC management (when adverse actions affect a minority staff member) are as dumb and irrational as tossing the baby out with the bath water!

There are several documented instances where correctional staff have been caught selling drugs to prison inmates (which, if convicted, is a felony offense); however, these people remain peace officers.

There are currently ongoing investigations that accuse numerous correctional officers of smuggling drugs into state prisons and selling them to inmates. These *investigations* will eventually *die a slow death* because CDC does its own investigations and CDC, **"takes care of its own!"** Sadly, the great majority of these krooked kops will remain and retain their peace officers status.

It is well known that within the California Department of Corrections, there is an appreciative number of peace officers who have been involved in domestic violence - some repeatedly. These people, too, will remain peace officers which makes an openly mockery of our current laws. Why do we continue to have *unenforceable* laws? Or, could it simply be just another example of our laws which apply to some and not all?

Correctional staff have been arrested for offenses ranging from soliciting prostitution to unholstering and firing their weapon during either a bar-room brawl or a domestic incident. They, too, remain peace officers. How about the prison warden who was hired while having three felony DUI convictions; or the parole agent who falsified state documents (that are routinely subjected to court review) relative to his mandatory home visits.

Maybe, we should consider the parole agent supervisor who, on three separate occasions, physically attacked, struck and injured a female parole agent. Oddly, this *supervisor* (if you choose to call him that) received a demotion that resulted in a salary increase. Figure that one out. This can only happen in the California Department of Corrections. CDC, have you no shame? Obviously, not.

The disproportionate numbers of Black peace officers who receive adverse actions compared to their White peers are alarming! White peace officers have been known to commit atrocious crimes including felonies; however, they retained their peace status. In fact, many of their crimes are intentionally unreported.

I vividly recall one individual (while assigned to Folsom State Prison), who wanted so badly to fire his weapon that he would frequently enter the gun rail (where the gunner was positioned), when his duties required him to be on the floor. This same officer found it necessary to fire his weapon on the prison yard to separate two inmates involved in a physical altercation.

I was the other officer assigned to the Control Room; however, I was responsible for providing gun coverage to the officers on the floor. Of interest, to me, was the fact that I neither heard the officer give a verbal warning nor did I hear him chamber a round in his weapon. All I heard were shots fired! This leaves me to believe that the officer had (against policy) *pre-chambered* his weapon.

It is CDC *policy* that a *warning* be given before firing any weapon (unless there is an immediate, life-threatening situation). The chambering of one's weapon is, therefore, considered a *warning*.

The California Department of Corrections (like most American companies) recruits its employees from the vast wealth of our Nation's workforce; therefore, it should come as no surprise that a *small **(but, significant)*** minority of its personnel come into the Department with their own *personal* and *hidden agendas*. It is *widely known* throughout CDC that *some* of its **White employees openly recruit new members into the Ku Klux Klan on State time**, giving **KKK** medallions (like the one depicted in this Chapter) to prospective (correctional staff) candidates at State institutions. While I am uncertain, this k*landestine re*k*ruitment* k*ampaign* may have also included convicted White felons.

These, *"good woods"* (White correctional officers) eventually become correctional sergeants, correctional lieutenants, correctional captains, parole agents, managers, supervisors, administrators......I think you get the picture.

Have I simply become paranoid or, is it even *remotely possible* that one of those, *"good woods"* was in the position to either influence or effect my termination from State Service? The answer may surprise you. Could it also be CDC management's *rationale* for repeatedly

iN tHE cAR

advising me that, *"a fair and equitable solution"* was agreed upon? Remember, even paranoiacs have enemies.

"Fair and equitable." I must once again ask this question: By whose standards? What yardstick of measurement and precedence were used to make that, *"fair and equitable"* determination? Again, I offer no answers; I only have questions.

Now, I am not implying that *everything* negative that happens to a Black person is unjustified. I am suggesting, however, that *everything* is **not** always as it appears to be. I honestly believe that:

♦♦♦

"In our imperfect world, perfect solutions are not merely elusive; they simply do not exist."

Lonnie F. DeWitt

♦♦♦

Unless we are willing to fully explore all available options, however, we will clearly shirk our inherent responsibilities and miss other golden opportunities. We are truly our *Brother's Keeper.* Therefore, it is imperative that we continue to remain vigilant throughout our Watch.

It is crucial for us to fully appreciate and understand that a person need not be a full-fledged, card-carrying **KKK-puke** to maintain that mentality. Truth be told, being White is clearly **not** a prerequisite.

Similarly, when I hear the derogatory word, "nigger," I do not get too upset. I merely consider the source. Just as a person need not be White to be a **KKK** member (or, have that mentality), a person need not be of Color to be a, "nigger." In America, we have more White niggers than Black ones!

These medallions are exquisitely designed - like a new Silver Dollar - giving the appearance of a United States Mint-look. Each medallion is *.999 pure one ounce Fine Silver.* That is reflected on the face of the medallion.

Incidentally, the numbers *"999"* when read upside down reflect the infamous **"666"** - **"the mark of the beast"** (Revelation 13:18). Of course, I am sure that this is purely coincidental. Yeah, right!

The following inscriptions appear on the *face* of each medallion:

KU KLUX KLAN

(a picture of a **burning cross** also appears on the left side of the medallion; in the center of the medallion is a **hood** with two eye-holes; and to the right are the numbers, **"1990"**).

The following inscriptions also appear on the *back* of each medallion:

KU KLUX KLAN
Unite,
America Into
One Order
Under One
Banner
.999 Pure 1 oz. Fine Silver

I cannot possibly be convinced that **everyone** in CDC management was totally unaware that this kind of *activity* existed *behind the walls* of our State penal institutions. Both Hoover® and Oreck® would envy this kind of powerful, self-contained vacuum. But, I will unequivocally state that had those **KKK** medallions been **Black Panther** medallions, there would be a host of *(former)* Black correctional staff in the unemployment line!

iN tHE cAR

How about the **senior CDC official** who, while in his office and in the presence of others, made the statement, **"What do those niggers want now?"** He was referring to Black parole agents. Hopefully, you will not be too shocked to learn that one of the, *"good woods"* who witnessed that conversation (yet, remained silent) was also one of the, *"good woods"* involved in my dismissal action. Please forgive me if I seem somewhat uncomfortable in having a, *"good wood"* to **objectively** evaluate the merits of my case.

Now, America, *don't even try* to **act** so surprised. During this past decade, other major United States corporations and business executives have made similar racial slurs either in public, during business meetings, or in memorandums (Texaco and Sacramento Cable - just to name a few).

Consider the incident where two correctional staff - one White and the other Black – who were carpooling together. One day, while on their way to work, they developed vehicle problems. The Black staff elected to stay with the disabled vehicle while the White staff walked to a nearby telephone to inform institutional supervisors that the two of them would be a little late for work because of vehicle problems.

The Black staff was later reprimanded and received a Letter of Instruction (for failing to notify his supervisor of vehicle difficulties that necessitated his being late for work). The other staff was *unaffected* by management's negative reaction (which is frequently the case when issues affect White correctional staff).

How about the Correctional Sergeant who had been separated from the military for two and a half years yet, during that time, he fraudulently absented himself from correctional duties while claiming *his, "two weeks of annual military reserve training."*

During that time, this Sergeant also claimed and received a week off each month to, *"attend military reserve training."* Once exposed, the Sergeant was demoted to a Correctional Officer.

That *demotion*, of course, allowed him to retain his peace officer status.

Now, one may clearly see just how *konvenient* it is for a White korrektional staff to commit either a serious misdemeanor or even a felony and *still* retain his/her peace officer status. That System, apparently, still believes that it's, **"OK"** to look the other way when one has the *right* **Komplexion** to make the **Konnection**.

Please believe that this "National Order of Klassic Kowardly Koneheads" not only exists in this sickly triage **(CDC - SPB - CCPOA)** but it is more widespread and prevalent throughout the State of California than one may choose to believe.

White law enforcement officers (in and out of the California Department of Corrections) will *jokingly* advise other White officers to "Dial (or radio-in) 3-11 **[three eleven]** if there is a *problem* that they can't handle!"

The letter **"K"** just happens to be the eleventh letter in our English alphabet. Now, let's *do the math*. **Three K's** (or, three eleven - 3 times 11 - therefore, conveniently becomes **three K's** or, **KKK**.

There are written volumes of indisputable evidence connecting White peace officers with committing racially motivated hate crimes.

Numerous White law enforcement personnel across the United States have developed their own racist codes like:

"UNIT"

which *secretly* means *U*nwanted (or *U*nwelcomed) *N*igger *I*n *T*own!

We're talking about some real sick puppies that, like a well-known retired White Los Angeles police detective, openly utter racial slurs while *hiding* behind a badge.

This self-verbalized **'N'-word** is used throughout the California Department of Corrections (especially within correctional institutions) as if it were the official induction of White staff into manhood through some sort of **sick rites of passage ritual**.

Unlike *many* American companies, however, the California Department of Corrections has opted to **look the other way**. Could this be yet another form of **passive acceptance**?

Yes, the California Department of Corrections has shamefully failed to learn its lessons in **Racism 101.** That Child Development Center was probably either being breast-fed or having recess when that course was given.

I felt that even the *modified* Adverse Action was still much too severe to impose upon me for a first-time *offense* (if you choose to call it that); especially, given the mild-to-no actions taken against non-Black parole agents who were involved in much more serious offenses.

I, therefore, appealed to the State Personnel Board in my April 25, 1994 letter:

◆ ◆ ◆

Dear Board Members:

On 12-14-93, I received notice, "Advisory of Intent to Conduct an Investigatory Interview." The letter stated, "allegations of undue familiarity have been made.

This interview will concern your possible violation of California Administrative Code Director's Title 15, Section 3400 (undue familiarity)."

When I agreed to discuss the allegations, without benefit of counsel/representation, it was with my understanding that I was being interviewed regarding my "possible violation of California Administrative Code Director's Title 15, Section 3400 (undue familiarity" as clearly expressed in my Advisory of Intent letter.

If I were to be questioned and subsequently charged regarding other perceived violations, then I should have been so advised at the onset of my interview; and, not upon my receipt of an Adverse Actions letter.

I, therefore, respectfully submit to this Board that my Correctional Peace Officers Bill of Rights have been clearly violated! During my Skelly Hearing, I took issue that effectively omitted/deleted several inappropriate comments and proliferated charges that necessitated an "amended" adverse action. It's interesting to note, however, that the lone charge (Section 3400) in which I was held to answer has yet to be addressed!

Instead, the real issues have been clouded through innuendoes and unsubstantiated "facts."

Please be advised that Section 3400 (Familiarity) states:

"Employees must not engage in undue familiarity with inmates, parolees, or the family of inmates or the family and friends of inmates or parolees. Whenever there is reason for an employee to have personal contact or discussions with an inmate or parolee or the family and friends of inmates and parolees, the employee must maintain a helpful but professional attitude and demeanor. Employees must not discuss their personal affairs with any inmate or parolee."

In remaining focused on the issues and elements that comprise Section 3400, let's discuss the word "undue" which means "excessive" or "disproportionate". In my April 4, 1994, letter to my Deputy Regional Administrator, Ms. Deborah Sager, I stated, "Admittedly, however, when she (Cathy) advised me of her husband's CDC-status, our "relationship" was severed (with the exception of isolated conversations and (very public) and brief contact).

I am confident that this Board may clearly discern between frequent/infrequent and excessive/inexcessive. Again, my isolated contacts with Cathy (upon my having knowledge that she was married to an inmate) neither falls within the meaning of "excessive" nor "disproportionate".

Further, I am also certain that this Board will appreciate that my (post-knowledge) contacts with Cathy clearly met the requirements demanded of Section 3400, in that I "maintained a helpful but professional attitude and demeanor." Again, I invite the Board's attention to my April 4, 1994, letter to Ms. Sager in which I stated, "I even asked her (Cathy) to "be patient and supportive" of her husband. As a friend, I would give this advice to anyone; and, I would challenge anyone to take a negative issue with my position!

While I cannot speak for each of you Board members, I place enormous value on personal friendship. When I enter into a friendship, I accept that friendship with an unconditional, positive regard that demands a two-party commitment.

In the case with Cathy and me, our friendship was sealed for nearly one year with a strong bond of mutual admiration before the "bomb" was dropped. The "bomb," of course, was Cathy's revelation to me that her husband was in prison and soon to be paroled! Nonetheless, when Cathy was stranded due to vehicular mechanical problems, she telephoned me for assistance and I responded (in my personal car and on my personal time).

While I will not apologize for my helping a friend in need, I will admit that I will, most assuredly, handle any similar situation with much more discretion.

Given my more than twenty-three years of honorable military service coupled with nearly five years of (heretofore unblemished) State service, I could certainly argue that it's virtually inconceivable that I would "suddenly" lack the necessary discipline to objectively perform my duties as a peace officer. How absurd!

I am confident that this Board, upon fully evaluating the totality of this entire (unfortunate) incident and, upon considering the merits of my written/verbal presentation(s), will reach an objective and totally unbiased decision.

Sincerely, Lonnie F. DeWitt

◆ ◆ ◆

While I was undergoing this entire administrative process, and clearly well before the State Personnel Board rendered its final determination, CJ elected to include this *isolated incident* in my employee evaluation. He subsequently gave me an *Unsatisfactory* rating in *Analytical Skills* because I failed to, *"adequately analyze the situation."*

The State Personnel Board upheld the Adverse Action taken against me. On the date of my hearing, the State's attorney included an additional specification; and although neither my attorney nor I had previously received notification (as required, by law), the Administrative Law Judge allowed its inclusion. To this day, I have yet to receive my copy of that document; therefore, I am unable to adequately address its contents.

Significantly underscoring the impact of the Administrative Law Judge's decision, is the fact that the State Personnel Board had a

mandatory duty to hold my hearing and render its decisions in accordance with the statutory mandates of Government Codes §§ 19578 and 19583. **Furthermore, Government Codes §§ 19578, 19583 and 18671.1 impose a mandatory obligation which is not discretionary to the State Personnel Board:**

❖❖❖

"SPB FAILURE TO HOLD A HEARING AND/OR RENDER A DECISION WITHIN THE MANDATORY TIME FRAMES SET FORTH RESULTS IN LOSS OF JURISDICTION. SAID FAILURE INVALIDATES AND REVOKES THE ADVERSE ACTION."

❖❖❖

Although the State Personnel Board **failed to comply with the aforementioned Government Codes** (since it failed to act in a "timely manner") and I fully apprised my attorney of this fact, **the SPB continued with this illegal hearing and disregarded the statutory requirements of our Government Codes.**

When I questioned my attorney regarding the Board's obviously blatant disregard for Government Codes, he simply shrugged and indicated that the California State Personnel Board *routinely* ignored those statutory requirements.

This Adverse Action was of the *utmost importance* to the California Department of Corrections to substantiate that it had taken, *"progressive discipline"* against me; thereby, justifying its decision to terminate my employment from State Service.

State employees (especially minorities) are held *strictly accountable* to every applicable (and obscure) Government Code. Is the California State Personnel Board exempt from these same accountabilities? I think not; however, the SPB seems to *blatantly*

iN tHE cAR

and (apparently) *routinely* **violate** these Codes with absolute impunity and without obvious regard for any possible adverse repercussions. **Who and where is the *Gate Keeper*?**

I had an audience with the president of the local chapter of a somewhat well respected Black organization. When I described the problems that I were having, that *leader* told me, "Well, that's the way it is......" I tuned that *(CJ-mentality)* man totally out.

Please, don't tell me, "the way it is." Show me the way it should be. If it's wrong, let's get involved and help change, "the way it is" to make it right (the way it ought to be).

Tell me....I'll forget;
Show me....I'll remember;
Involve me....I'll understand.

I deeply love my Black people. We do have, however, a bunch of watered-down *so-called* **Black** organizations that are more interested in their own self-imaging (involving black-tie social functions) than in actively focusing on and helping to resolve real-life issues adversely affecting minorities.

Most CDC staff does not have the courage to speak out against a wrong that has taken place. I view their *combined conduct* as representing the *epitome of cowardice in the line of duty*.

There was an *incident* in the parole office one afternoon in which Janice Gaye became extremely angry and called *CJ* a, "bastard!" It never ceases to amaze me just how eager some of us (Black folk) are to fully accept and forgive degrading comments from *some* people and not *others*. We are so quick to put *each other* in *check* while allowing derogatory comments made by *some* to seemingly go unnoticed and clearly unchallenged.

While most CDC staff simply look forward to their next paycheck, there are those who seem to enjoy their antisocial behavioral tendencies, which are clearly characterized by their lack of moral and ethical growth. I certainly cannot change someone's attitude; however, I do hope that this book will effect a positive behavioral adjustment on behalf of CDC management.

It's truly unfortunate that some of these are officials who, while remaining hidden behind that entity known as the California Department of Corrections, use their positions of public trust to quite literally screw those who either oppose them or their (warped) views.

These managers will continue to be touched by a sickness, diagnosed as **Color-challenged**, which causes *severe integrity impairment*, unless properly treated.

Chapter Fifteen

The Olympian Set-up
(the mother of all set-ups)

While commuting from San Jose to Sacramento on May 17, 1994, I had the opportunity to assist the Tracy Police Department effect an arrest on Interstate 5. The following morning I mentioned the incident and of my involvement to Janice Gaye, Acting Unit Supervisor and to other Unit 5 parole agents.

At that time, Ms. Gaye stated, "Gawd, you ought to get accommodation fo dat [that's the way she talked]!"

That weekend, (May 21, 1994), I typed the following letter addressed to Sergeant Ventura of the Tracy Police Department:

Dear Sergeant Ventura:

On 5-17-94, at approximately 1730 hours, Tracy Police and the California Highway Patrol were involved in a high-speed chase of a vehicle traveling northbound on Interstate 5 (just North of Tracy).

I immediately joined in the pursuit and assisted on-scene law enforcement personnel in effecting a safe arrest.

I would very much appreciate a letter of commendation from either you or your superiors recognizing me for the actions that I took during those tense moments.

My actions taken, along with a "proposed" letter, are enclosed for your consideration.

It was a pleasure assisting your professional law enforcement team and helping them to effect a safe arrest.

Sincerely, Lonnie F. DeWitt

(Enclosure - My draft letter)

Dear Agent DeWitt:

It has come to my attention that on 5-17-94, you assisted my police officers and the California Highway Patrol in effecting an arrest of three individuals involved in a high-speed vehicle chase on northbound Interstate 5.

While driving northbound, you realized that an emergency was in progress and you immediately activated your "emergency flashers" while flashing your headlights to warn other unsuspecting motorists of the impending danger.

Once the Number 3 lane was clear of traffic, the speeding vehicle, along with the pursing police vehicles, was able to continue without causing a traffic mishap.

You then zigzagged your vehicle across all three lanes of the Interstate to effectively halt all northbound traffic. By doing this, you allowed a southbound CHP officer to effectively cross the median-divide and assist in the northbound pursuit without endangering any lives. Further, your actions in safely stopping all northbound traffic eliminated any vehicle fatalities involving on-scene law enforcement personnel and other motorists; and you effectively kept all traffic from the scene in the event that the use of weapons became necessary.

You then exited your vehicle, properly identified yourself, and assisted on-scene law enforcement personnel. I am advised that you personally "cleared" the vehicle (of other possible vehicle occupants) and gave the "all clear" sign allowing both Tracy police and CHP to fully concentrate on the three detainees.

Your personal and professional actions clearly represent the epitome of a dedicated law enforcement officer. Please accept my personal appreciation for a superior job well done!

Respectfully, (Blank)

On June 20, 1994, I was given the "Advisory of Intent to Conduct an Investigatory Interview" for my involvement in assisting the Tracy Police.

It then became clearly evident that I was on CDC's prime list to be *screwed*.

On June 23, 1994, I was interviewed regarding my off-duty involvement with the Tracy Police Department. During the interview I stated that I had mentioned my involvement (the very next day following the incident) to Ms. Janice Gaye, who was the Acting Unit Supervisor.

Prior to my interview I informed Ms. Gaye of my intentions to *go on record* that I had, in fact, mentioned this incident to her. I wanted to avoid her being surprised when she was questioned regarding our conversation. I silently thought, **"Good lookin' out."**

Steve subsequently interviewed Ms. Gaye and asked her **one** question regarding this incident:

Steve

My question is that you were apparently, from what I understand, the Acting Unit Supervisor of San Jose #5 on or about May 18, 1994, which I am going to guess was a Thursday or Friday, and I am told by Parole Agent -I Lonnie F DeWitt that in that capacity, as the Unit Supervisor, the Acting Unit Supervisor, he approached you on or about that date, but certainly after May 17, 1994 that he had participated in a police action in the Tracy area. Could you recollect any such conversation?"

Janice

"Well, first off, I am not really sure that I was the Acting Unit Supervisor on that particular day. I was just going through a list of memos from 1992 up through 1993 in which I was listed as Acting AUS and I usually keep those and I could not find any recent ones...that doesn't mean that there aren't any. First off, I question whether or not I was Acting Unit Supervisor that day. I do recall a conversation in which Lonnie DeWitt had mentioned to me about some police involvement; however, from what I recall of that conversation there was no mention of when, where, how. He mentioned, from what I could remember, about blocking, assisting them in blocking off traffic out on the highway; but, I am not sure. I don't know what agency and I don't know where.

He was not very specific and from what I can recall, it was in the middle of some other conversation where I know that I was not approached in the capacity of you are the Acting AUS I need to report to you. Lonnie was frequently coming into my office over the months telling me about things that were going on with him and like I said from what I can recall, it was...may have been in the middle of some other conversation as a kind of matter-of-factly, this is what happened and not only to mention that the first that this came to light I guess was on Monday when Lonnie came back from vacation.

Once again, he came into my office and said, "Look at these two letters that I received while I was on vacation". Acting AUS? No, just another conversation as far as I was concerned. These are two letters that I had written up. Do you believe this what they are doing to me now? And, that was kind of how the conversations had always been and he said I saw the letter in which he I guess had written up for not informing his supervisor about this incident that he was involved in, and I said yeah because I had recalled, you know, him mentioning it to me and he said, "yeah, you were the Acting AUS, remember when I told you that I had assisted the law enforcement agencies?" And, I don't even know if it was a vehicle accident or what kind of situation it was. There was no details asked, there was no details offered other than he had assisted a law enforcement agency. He had also mentioned that he had asked for or I told him, or I implied that he should get some letter of commendation, and I just looked at him and said, "What are you talking about?" And, what immediately come to mind was that I did recall saying something to the effect that did you get a letter of commendation, but that was again not knowing when this event had happened. It could have happened weeks or months before. There was no date mentioned and the specific reason why I had asked that was because we see the letters or the memo from Region all the time where people have been commended; people for various things like Ken Pulley was involved in a bank robbery; Michael Tung, when he was involved in something else, and that was my thought process. I would not and did not ask him to go get any letter of commendation. I know that I would not do that, in fact, I had had an involvement with the cocaine bust last September and I have had a conversation with CJ where I said you know I questioned having received something like that and he specifically told me that "don't worry about it, you know that is not something we solicit, it is basically not proper protocol." I had already knew that. I didn't get one, therefore, why would I ask him to go get one? So my thing was just an acknowledgment of whatever you are talking about, did anybody acknowledge it? So, that is the extent of my knowledge of any conversation or any involvement in this."

Every time I read that statement it makes me want to vomit! I can fully understand and appreciate that panic-stricken Janice probably felt somewhat threatened by the Investigatory Hearing; however, she did not have to sacrifice her integrity (if there were ever any) because of a perceived threat! I am grateful that she was asked *only* **one** question! I am reminded of a quote by the late Dr. Martin Luther King, Jr.:

"Many people fear nothing more terribly than to take a position which stands out sharply from the prevailing opinion. The tendency of most is to adopt a view that is so ambiguous that it will include everything and so popular that it will include everybody. We are called to be people of conviction, not conformity; of moral nobility; not social respectability. We are commanded to live differently and according to a higher loyalty."

At that moment, Janice became an active participant in my administrative circumcism where my surgery was *botched* by the *Master Butcher*, California Department of Corrections. There is a *big*

iN tHE cAR

difference between *circumcism* and *castration*! To this day, I harbor no ill feelings against Janice although she made her position quite clear to me when she stated, "I don't want to be involved in your mess!"

I then wrote another letter to Philip Isenberg on August 1, 1994, which read:

Dear Phil:

Thank you for your personal intervention into my dilemma as previously expressed in my May 18, 1994 letter to you.

Unfortunately, my situation not only remains unresolved, but is now complicated by management's overt attempt to discredit me through harassment and blatant retribution resulting from my letter to you!

I had the opportunity (while off-duty and traveling home from San Jose to Sacramento) to assist the Tracy Police Department in effecting the arrest of three individuals. On May 21, 1994, I wrote a letter to Sergeant Ventura, of the Tracy PD, outlining my efforts and asked that he consider writing me a letter of commendation for my efforts. I have enclosed a copy of my "proposed" letter of commendation to Sergeant Ventura and the cover letter for your review.

When I returned to work (after a scheduled week's vacation) on June 20, 1994, I discovered in my "in-basket" an envelope marked "Confidential" advising me of "Advisory of Intent to Conduct an Investigatory Interview" scheduled for June 23, 1994, for my actions in assisting the Tracy Police Department.

Please note, that as of the date of my investigatory interview, this situation remains "under investigation," which places undue stress in my professional working relationship. It appears that my Regional Administrator, Mr. Ronald Chow, has taken a personal vendetta against me (for my contacting you) and, is using his official position to cause irreparable harm - psychologically, financially and professionally - to me and my family.

My California Correctional Peace Officers Association (CCPOA) representative most aptly expressed Mr. Chow's position by stating:

**"Mr. Chow gives Adverse Actions
where other Regional Administrators
give Commendations!"**

I neither need nor deserve this kind of "job-related" stress. I can no longer trust management in its present "retaliatory posture" to make the right decisions regarding my welfare.

I therefore, again, respectfully request your personal intervention to effect my immediate transfer to Sacramento. It is imperative that I attend to the emotional needs of my family and begin the "healing process" of my own "job-related" trauma!

Sincerely, Lonnie F. DeWitt

The same day that I received the Advisory Intent, my Assistant Unit Supervisor, Kevin Shimira, placed a Memorandum in my *in-basket* where he had documented (while I was in Sacramento) my, "Improper Storage of Dangerous Evidence."

The *vultures* were beginning to salivate as they circled overhead! I felt their sharpened teeth dig into my squirming body. I tried to fight; but it's no use. There were just too many of them. "Et tu, Kevin?"

Kevin was *well off base* in his Memorandum and even though he later apologized, the *damage* had already been done. The *vultures* had already smelled the sweet scent of fresh *meat* and had begun to salivate as they tasted the blood that seeped from my gaping wounds. Yes, Kevin, it was much too late for an apology. A simple telephone call would have been the professional (and *manly*) thing to do.

I then wrote Pete Wilson, the Governor of California. I wanted Governor Wilson to be *personally aware* of that CDC-orchestrated *unleveled playing field*. I knew that Pete could care less; however, it

iN tHE cAR

was a *necessary evil* for him to be included in my *documentation*.

My August 29, 1994, letter to Pete Wilson read:

Dear Governor Wilson:

It has been nearly 17 months (April 13, 1993) since my wife suffered an aneurysm and I have repeated tried to effect a transfer, based on this bonafide hardship condition, from the San *Jose Parole office to an office in the Sacramento Area (my permanent residence), as a State Parole Agent-1.*

The attached documents will provide you with a clear background of the steps that I have taken to effect my transfer and the steps that management has taken to disregard my family's personal and medical hardships.

While I am not writing you to either point fingers or assign blame; hopefully, you will hold Parole and Community Services Division management personally accountable for its inactions and apparent insensitivity for one of its staff members. For instance, ask management to justify its position in recently transferring several parole agents (without hardships), to Sacramento, without acknowledging my hardship request!

Management has clearly shown contempt and callousness toward me and my family problems, which causes me personal frustration and professional degradation.

How may we possibly expect management to render impartial and fair judgments to the people we are charged to supervise - both inmates and parolees - when management is either incapable or unwilling to satisfactorily resolve its staff issues?

Further, upon reading my entire package, one may clearly understand why there is such a disproportionate number of minority staff (especially, Blacks) receiving Adverse Actions (when compared with our non-Black counterparts).

Governor, my primary concern, however, is for you to become personally involved in my dilemma and to effect my immediate transfer to a Sacramento parole office as a case-carrying parole agent (my current position); and, for you to ensure that I do not receive any retribution for corresponding to you.

I do realize, that as Governor of our State, that you have greater priorities that involve a much larger spectrum; therefore, I will be available to discuss the merits of my letter with any of your staff.

Sincerely, Lonnie F. DeWitt

On Monday morning, September 7, 1994, when I returned to work (following my weekend off), I was busy drafting my parolees' annual reviews when *CJ* walked by (on his way to his office). As usual, I spoke; however, this particular morning, I received no response. About fifteen to twenty minutes later, *CJ* stopped by my office and said, "Steve [South Bay District Administrator] wants to see us in his office." I said, "OK," and we both walked downstairs together into Steve Scheller's office.

Steve handed me my Notice of Adverse Action and advised me that my dismissal from State Service was effective on September 14, 1994 - in seven days. Steve told me that he did not agree with the action taken against me; *CJ* said nothing! I was then advised that I needed to have all of my equipment turned-in and my desk cleaned out, "by close of business" on September 14, 1994. Shortly thereafter, Steve told me that I could, "go home" if I wanted to and that he would charge me, "sick leave for four hours."

It was an eerie feeling as I began my premature (260-mile) round-trip home. Although I had just become the newest *casualty* in that scandalous CDC triangle (*who you know; who you owe; who you blow*) still, I somehow felt that a huge weight had been lifted from my shoulders.

I had dared to look the beast in the eyes; and at that point I fully understood its nature. The beast. It could very well be the Black descendant of a stool pigeon; an overzealous Asian descendant of a second generation immigrant; the Spanish descendant of a bandolero;

the descendant of a carcajou; the Chinese or Indian descendant of a da coit; or, the White descendant of a former slave owner. The beast. It showed no shame in its game as it glared back at me with that lean and hungry look. My k*rash* k*ourse* in **American Racism 666** had begun.

Although my mind remained free while I had been shackled and held hostage for seventeen months, my body was still imprisoned by a System that I once revered and trusted to *do the right thing.*

With its Machiavellian tactics and unconscionable treatment of minority staff, that System was determined to destroy me because I dared to question its discriminatory policies and decisions.

I am honored to join my Black brothers and sisters who have likewise faced and fought this same sinister kreature that has somehow disguised itself as a respectable State entity:

California Department of Corrections

aka: California Department of Corruption
aka: California Department of Censorship
aka: Child Development Center

Two months later, on October 31, 1994, I received the following response from Governor Wilson's office. By then, of course, the California Department of Corrections had already terminated me, (with Pete Wilson's blessings, I am sure) pending my administrative appeal:

Dear Mr. DeWitt:

Thank you for your letter expressing your concerns regarding your requests to the California Department of Corrections' management for an employee hardship transfer. As the Governor's Chief Deputy Legal Affairs Secretary, I have been asked to respond.

We understand from your letter that your wife suffered an aneurysm in 1993 and since that time you have sought a transfer from your assignment as a parole agent in San Jose to a position here in

Sacramento. We also note that several alternative employment suggestions were offered, as well as an explanation of an existing agreement with CCPOA regarding transfers and rehires.

We have, however, received recent information from the Department advising us that you were the subject of an administrative action resulting in termination from State service. In light of this development, it would be inappropriate for the Governor to comment. At this point, we can only offer good wishes for your wife's recovery.

Thank you for bringing this matter to the Governor's attention.

Sincerely, Patricia C. Esgro

How silly of me! The Governor *appointed* the Director for the California Department of Corrections. We cannot logically expect the Governor to find fault with the person whom he appointed; now, can we? This California Governor has a history of not only appointing unqualified people; but, he also has a distasteful record of publicly supporting their lack of integrity and resulting mismanagement.

Tyrant Pete continues to rule Californians who are beyond the *stage of denial*! It seems that many Californians are in the *acceptance stage* where they have become comfortable and complacent while occasionally grunting, **"…well, that's the way it is…!"**

In my letter to Pete, I asked him to, "become personally involved in my dilemma…." It's quite obvious, to me, that he did. I no longer have *that* dilemma.

California's infamous storm system of 1997, known as *El Niño*, *ain't got shit* on *El Peteō*, who has reeked havoc throughout Southern, Central and Northern California for far too long.

It is now time for Pete to perform his **k**otillion march and come out of the **k**loset and allow us to view the **real** Pete Wilson. The *former* **KKK** Grand Dragon-turned-politician did; and as we saw, he was greeted with open arms. *El Peteō* should follow suit. I am sure that he'll find Californians truly empathetic people.

The *real good* news that I will offer about the Wilson administration is: **"Thank the good Lord for term limits!"** Although a review court initially ruled that the imposition of terms was, "unconstitutional," a higher court ruled to the contrary. I wonder if our courts will, one day, rule that *axploitation* is also *"unconstitutional!"*

In my opinion, Pete and his cronies (including his *Oreo side-kick, W.C.*) simply got a *jump-start* on the infamous California Civil Rights Initiative (CCRI), Proposition 209. They all played a passive role as I was being illegally terminated from State Service and replaced by a, *"good wood."*

I sort of understand the sick mentalities and hidden agendas of that Administration which suffers from political orgasm of grinding inertia. Therefore, the quote, **"Fire all the Blacks and replace 'em with Whites"** could just as easily been issued by a Kissing Kousin from that sleazy Administration.

For the misinformed, that bold **statement** is nothing *new*. Officials in the upper echelons of Corporate America have openly expressed similar views and statements.

The former executive of Sacramento Cable, within days of his arrival in 1990, issued a directive to **"fire all the niggers."** The, **"Black jelly bean"** racial slurs made by Texaco executives and the racial slurs made by Bob Crumpler, owner of Nissan dealerships in Newport News and Portsmouth, Virginia - where he referred to a Black American maintenance worker as a, "nigger" - simply help reinforce White America's reluctance to fully accept Black Americans as their equal.

I applaud Nissan Motor Corporation, USA for canceling its franchise agreement with Crumpler following his *unfortunate* remarks.

Yes, **American racism** is alive and well as we (people of Color) continue to play on a very unleveled playing field. The sad reality is that bigots and bigotry will continue to flourish unless each of us take an active role in recognizing racism and tearing it from its roots.

My subsequent administrative (Skelly) hearing with Ron Chow was nothing short of an *administrative joke*. My replacement was already in place and my termination was a *done deal*.

At the onset of my hearing, Ron Chow looked at me and asked, "Do I have to beat you in the head with a baseball bat to get your attention?" I simply replied, "You already have!" At the close of my hearing, Ron Chow then sarcastically advised me to, "Just stay home and take care of your wife!"

I knew then that Ron Chow *had already* decided to terminate my employment from State Service, without objectively evaluating the merits of my oral presentation. His decision to terminate me from State Service - based on my *Good Samaritan* act - defies common sense. But, then again, *that* is exactly what I have learned to expect from CDC management.

"A rose, by any other name ……..."

"Discrimination (racism), by any other name ……."

No, America, freedom is NOT really free!

Chapter Sixteen

Conspiracy of Silence

p steps the State Personnel Board (SPB) - the administrative watchdog for the State of California! This Board has sole responsibility to act as the overseer in administrative actions involving State employees. Therefore, the Administrative Law Judge (ALJ) who hears each case is ethically obligated to render an objective opinion to the Board for its decision. But, what happens when there is an **ethics breakdown** in this System?

What other immediate and inexpensive recourse do State employees have to ensure that they receive fair and impartial hearings? None. Or, at least, there are *no publicized alternatives*.

It is absolutely essential that you understand this administrative process to fully appreciate my frustrations and those of other State employees who have also faced this Board that continues to act with absolute impunity while dispensing *Just Us*.

During this process, the State's attorney asked me if I would agree to accept another CDC position that offered my same salary - in other than a peace officer status. I agreed.

Both attorneys (mine and the State's) then gave me a *golden rod* - a comprehensive listing of all CDC vacant positions - and asked that I select three choices in which I was qualified (based on my education, experiences and current salary). They both stated that I would be given one of my three choices and that I would, *"soon"* be back to work.

My attorney told me that because the State's attorney was in my, *"corner"* that I had a 99.99% chance of regaining immediate State employment - in other than a peace officer position. At that time, I told my attorney that I was more concerned with the .01%.

My concerns were later validated as the State reneged on its verbal agreement - at the eleventh hour - to me. The reason that the State's attorney gave me was because of, "logistics" CDC could not (or, simply stated, *would not*) place me in another position. The California Department of Corrections made it quite clear that it **did not want me back in any capacity** (not even as a janitor).

That golden rod was instantly (as though by magic) transformed into an iron shaft through a reversed (and perverted) alchemy process. You need not guess where they stuck it!

This *drive-through kangaroo court* (also known as the State Peckerwood Board) offers neither relief nor sanctuary to minority members facing administrative actions. I quickly learned that I was *totally ill-prepared* to face an Administrative Law Judge whose objectivity left much to be desired. Consider, for instance, the *opening remarks* of the ALJ who, in my case on June 6, 1995, stated

iN tHE cAR

quite adamantly:

♦ ♦ ♦

> "If what I've read is true, it is likely that I will rule in favor of the State; and it would be in your best interest to settle!"

♦ ♦ ♦

Now, I ask, *"Who's zoomin' who?"* How was I expected to receive an impartial hearing, given the ALJ's *opening remarks*?

I had prepared the following letter for the ALJ's review; however, **I was not given the opportunity to present it.**

♦ ♦ ♦

Dear Ms. Bunker:

Over the past five years, the California Department of Corrections has been very good to me – both professionally and financially. So good, in fact, that I encouraged my son, Lonnie Jr., to pursue a career with the Department. My son is now a Correctional Officer at Donovan State Correctional Facility in San Diego.

During my 2-½ year tenure as a parole agent, I worked an average 12- to 14-hour workday. My personal and professional desire and commitment to excel as a parole agent far exceeded any financial benefits and demands for compensatory overtime payments (as funds were simply not available). I merely wanted to excel in my chosen profession and share my wealth of experiences with my peers, my clients and my community.

On April 13, 1993, my 25th wedding anniversary, my wife suffered an aneurysm that required her immediate hospitalization in the intensive care unit at Kaiser Foundation Hospital in Sacramento. I repeatedly asked Parole and Community Services Division to effect my transfer from the San Jose office to one in either the Sacramento or Stockton area, to give me the opportunity to attend to my wife's medical and psychological needs.

Unfortunately, my requests - that included numerous oral and written presentations - were ignored by the Division for 17 months following my wife's medical emergency.

In my quest to be heard by an impartial party, I then wrote several letters outside of the Division requesting intervention in this matter. One may argue that my persistence in requesting a hardship transfer and my letters outside the Division may have embarrassed our managers to the point that my dismissal became necessary; and that my assisting another law enforcement agency, while off-duty, merely became a vehicle to effect that dismissal. Still, it's difficult for me to explain to my 11-year old daughter who, with teary eyes, asked, "Dad, why did you stop and help those cops, anyway?"

My actions, while neither criminal, immoral, nor malicious, were precipitated merely by my concerns and fears for the safety of the on-scene officers. Unfortunately, my proactive and "good faith" concerns cost me my job! While I refuse to point fingers or assign blame, I honestly believe, however, that I have been unlawfully dismissed by Parole and Community Services Division.

I, therefore, respectfully beseech this Board to carefully and objectively consider the merits of this case and to reach a conclusion that would allow me to rejoin my peers and continue my career as a State Parole Agent, without delay; thereby, helping to minimize further financial and emotional hardships that the DeWitt family has suffered these past several months.

Thank you for allowing me to make these few remarks and for your empathetic consideration in these proceedings.

Sincerely, Lonnie F. DeWitt

There was no administrative hearing! I was literally browbeaten into a Stipulation for Settlement. I was administratively bullied.

The principles of logic suggest that one *cannot* and *should not* make a **deal with the devil** and expect to win. That is *clearly* a **lose-lose** *proposition*. I violated that principle and settled. I lost.

On September 7, 1995, I wrote the Attorney General of the United States, Ms. Janet Reno:

◆ ◆ ◆

Dear Ms. Reno:

I beg you to thoroughly investigate the contents of my letter which addresses some serious legal and discriminatory issues within the California Department of Corrections (CDC) and the Parole and Community Division (P&CSD).

Both CDC and P&CSD have repeatedly shown its hostile contempt and benign and deliberate indifference toward me, my family, and other minority staff. It was because of that indifference and contempt that I was dismissed from State Service as a Parole Agent.

Although my dismissal was supposedly based on, "misconduct" it was, in reality, based on letters that I wrote to my elected representatives describing my grievances with the Department of Corrections. In other words, my Constitutional First Amendment rights were clearly violated and my employment was subsequently terminated!

Ms. Reno, this entire scenario regarding my dismissal is shrouded with serious administrative and legal irregularities by Department managers who manipulated an incident and "created" false parameters to effect my dismissal. **The Department has managed to reduce a highly disciplined, honorably retired Air Force veteran of twenty-three years into an individual who now has less rights than a convicted felon!**

I have been given a persona non grata status by an extremely insensitive and vindictive system.

Ms. Reno, I've traveled extensively worldwide and I have never suffered the personal and professional indecencies and degradation as I have with the California Department of Corrections and its "good ole boy" system.

I have not only been victimized and "railroaded," I have literally been "black-balled" from an entire department - the department which is obligated the largest budget in the State of California - the California Department of Corrections and the Youth Authority! It is shameful, at best, to think that a convicted murderer (or any felon), can serve time in prison; be released on parole; violate the conditions of parole; return to prison; and again, be released on parole. Finally, upon attaining the maximum parole limits, be released into the community.

This person is then eligible to accept employment with CDC (in a non-peace officer position) - however, because I have been irrevocably ostracized from the Department, I cannot accept ANY position within the California Department of Corrections or the Youth Authority, as I am no longer "welcomed!"

Shame on CDC for outwardly showing its contempt and openly continuing its "fine tradition" toward institutional racism. Now, Ms. Reno, please ask yourself, was I merely being disciplined or was I, quite frankly, destroyed!

Many, many fine peace officers commit infractions much more serious than mine; yet, some go "unnoticed" (unreported) while others receive much less harsher punishment. For instance, consider the parole agent who knowingly and repeatedly falsified official parolee case file documents. As you are aware, these documents must, by law, be current and accurate, as they are often requested by court subpoena. This officer, however, remains employed as a State Parole Agent! Obviously, this officer's identity is not an issue. What is an issue is the obvious manner in which CDC management elects to do business - extremely subjectively!

It appears that objectivity has no place in CDC; and unfortunately, Black staff who are disciplined, receive much harsher "penalties" than their non-Black counterparts.

My dismissal was effected by RONALD CHOW, Regional II Administrator, who was far removed from my daily working environment. Yet, CHOW, while having no direct observation of me

iN tHE cAR

or my professional working demeanor and, without support from my supervisors, made the decision to terminate my employment. It is painfully obvious that CHOW's decision was precipitated by my letters - (see attachments 1 through 13) - rather than by the "actions" that I took on May 17, 1994.

In fact, CHOW could find no legal basis with which to terminate my employment unless my actions were considered "on-duty." So, CHOW did the next best thing - he manipulated the playing field and expanded the parameters to reflect that I was on-duty when I stopped and assisted the Tracy Police Department to effect an arrest on Interstate 5, which was 60 miles away from the parole office!

The Department of Corrections Administrative Bulletin 93/33, dated July 28, 1993, clearly and unquestionably dictates the parameters and conditions when a parole agent is determined to be on-duty (attachment 14). These eight established criterion fully substantiate my position that my actions took place, while in an off-duty capacity; therefore, I was not subject to the constraints established by the Department of Corrections for its parole agents, who, while on-duty, offer to provide mutual assistance to other law enforcement personnel.

There simply is no statutory requirement for any parole agent to report the unholstering of his/her firearm, while off-duty. While on-duty, however, parole agents are required to comply with the Department of Corrections Operations Manual, Chapter 80000, Section 86010, "P&CSD Weapons Policy (attachment 15), which states: *A parole agent will make a verbal report to their immediate supervisor, whenever the firearm is drawn from its holder in the course of duty. A written report will be submitted through channels to the Deputy Director P&CSD headquarters so as to arrive no later than the 20th calendar day following the date of the unholstering incident."*

There is a proposal to eliminate the requirement for parole agents to report the unholstering of weapons on-duty because many parole agents and their supervisors tend to ignore this time consuming and administrative requirement.

The Department of Corrections Operations Manual, Chapter 80000, Subchapter 86000, Section 86010, "P&CSD Weapons Policy" (attachment 16), further states, "...Parole Agents who choose to carry a privately owned firearm while off-duty, whether or not the firearm is carried in a concealed manner, do so at their own risk, and in doing so, assume the same liability as any other private citizen so armed." I continue to maintain that I assumed that risk as a private citizen when I stopped to assist Tracy Police.

Even the California Correctional Peace Officers' Association (CCPOA) acknowledged that I was ineligible for CCPOA legal representation because my actions resulted from my off-duty conduct beyond the scope of my employment.

It is truly inconceivable to even imagine that I was dismissed from State Service as a State Parole Agent simply because I stopped and assisted the Tracy Police effect an arrest while in an off-duty capacity! To this day, I have extreme difficulty in rationalizing CHOW's decision; except, that it was based purely on personalities ("argumentum adhominem") and not the issues involved. The message is quite clear: "Don't question RONALD CHOW's authority!"

There was simply no legal precedence with which CHOW made his decision to terminate my employment. In fact, California courts have previously ruled (and upheld) that a correctional officer who is cited for Driving Under the Influence of Alcohol (DUI) while off-duty, cannot be further punished by CDC.

Therefore, if Tracy Police felt that I acted improperly as a private citizen when I stopped to assist, then that agency had one year to file a criminal complaint against me with their respective district attorney. The absence of that complaint clearly suggests that my "assistance" to them was not an issue.

In fact, at no time did Tracy Police contact CDC and complain about me. CDC learned of my involvement, only because I shared my experience with other office staff, one of whom was the Acting Unit Supervisor.

That weekend (while off-duty), I typed a letter (attachment 17) asking Tracy police to consider me for some type of recognition for my personal efforts in assisting them and, I included a draft proposal (outlining my involvement). CDC then, upon learning of this, initiated all contacts with Tracy Police and subsequently concocted this unleveled "playing field" and terminated my employment four months following the incident.

There is really a dichotomy to this entire scenario. On the one hand, CDC has taken a negative position by my off-duty involvement in assisting another law enforcement agency. Yet, on the other hand, while at the parole academy, we were taught and, in fact, given literature addressing Penal Code 150: "Refusing to Aid Officers in Arrest" (attachment 18). That code states: "Any peace officer may require any "able bodied person above 18 years of age" to come to their aid and assistance while making an arrest (posse comitatus). Failure to come to the assistance of a uniformed peace officer can result in a fine of not less than $50 nor more than $1,000. This statute does not seem to require a specific request for assistance; i.e., the law states "neglecting or refusing" to assist. Therefore, it appears that if a citizen (able bodied and over 18) observed a uniformed officer in need of assistance, that person is obligated to come to his or her aid absent a specific request." (Highlighted for emphasis only).

On June 6, 1995 at 9:00 A.M., I was scheduled for an administrative State Personnel Board (SPB) hearing. The Administrative Law Judge, BARBARA BUNKER, then advised that we would be "off-record". (Both she and I had our tape recorders off). At this point BUNKER asked me if I wanted to continue with the hearing or possibly settle the matter through mediation. I advised BUNKER that I did not want to negotiate and asked that we continue with the hearing.

BUNKER then stated, "If what I've read is true, it is likely that I will rule in favor of the State." I then replied that I was confident that my arguments would overwhelmingly convince the SPB that my actions did not warrant dismissal from State Service and that the SPB would rule in my favor. BUNKER then commented that even if she did rule in my favor that there was no guarantee that I would receive any retroactive financial benefits.

BUNKER went on to say that CDC would appeal her decision and that it would take "a couple of years" before it was resolved. I then questioned BUNKER about the authority (or, lack thereof) of the SPB and its decision if CDC were allowed the latitude to ignore that decision. BUNKER then stated that even if she did rule in my favor that she had no authority to state where I would be reassigned; adding that CDC would probably send me back to San Jose. I then stated that would be fine, I simply wanted my job.

BUNKER then asked that I leave the room while she, my attorney, the State's attorney and Curtis Jackson, my former supervisor, consulted.

Finally, my attorney exited and asked me what did it take for me to settle. I then stated, "My job as a Parole Agent." My attorney stated that was not possible as CDC has made it clear that it did not want me back in any capacity.

Ms. Reno, this dialogue went on and on and, quite frankly, I felt that I had been browbeaten! I told my attorney that I was experiencing extreme financial difficulty (as I had been without employment for seven months).

Finally, with the help of BUNKER, my attorney convinced me that it would be in the "best interest of all parties" concerned if I settled; and, by doing so, I would then be immediately eligible to seek further State employment.

Unfortunately, that was not true. On 9/22/95, I received a letter (attachment 19), which essentially stated that I needed to have written approval from the SPB to compete in one of many positions that I had previously sought! On 9/25/95, I contacted ROBERTA at the telephone given on the return address of this letter. ROBERTA then queried her computer and advised me that a Form "S41" had been attached to my files that indicated I had been terminated from state service because of adverse actions and that absent a letter from the SPB that I would be ineligible for State employment.

Obviously, this is certainly contrary to what my stipulation dictated!

CDC appears to have the latitude to act inappropriately and, in some instances, above the law. It certainly would be "nice" if CDC management were held responsible and accountable for both their actions and inactions!

CDC even failed to provide me with my check of $25,000.00 in "damages" in a timely manner, as mandated in the Stipulation for Settlement, which caused me both financial and emotional hardship.

Again, CDC does what it wants and when it wants with absolutely no accountability! It is apparent that CDC management lacks both structure and integrity.

Furthermore, I seriously question the tactics of the SPB. Is it the SPB's position to mediate/negotiate (browbeat) settlements or, is it the SPB's position to objectively listen, evaluate, and render an impartial decision? At the onset, it was apparent to me who the SPB represented! Incidentally, we did not "go on record" until that afternoon after both lawyers returned from lunch with draft copies of the Stipulation for Settlement!

I applaud U.S. District Judge Lawrence K. Karlton who, in a scalding 82-page order, advised CDC that he would "assume oversight and authority" over CDC's imprisoned mentally ill. Judge Karlton seriously reprimanded Pete Wilson and top CDC officials as having shown "deliberate indifference" to the unconstitutional conditions under which the imprisoned mentally ill exist.

The Judge went on to state that evidence of CDC's "knowledge of gross inadequacies in their system was overwhelming." I am elated to know that Judge Karlton was bold and caring enough to take a professional stance against such abuse.

Unfortunately, that is only the "tip of the iceberg," as, "gross inadequacies" and discriminatory practices are wide-spread throughout CDC; and for one to openly complain equates to "suicide" (as in my case)!

In closing, Ms. Reno, I will state that the California Department of Corrections has been very good to me -- both professionally and financially. Yes, the Department has its share of problems; however, most of those issues may be satisfactorily resolved if management would only take time to become more sensitive to the needs of its staff, inmate, and parolee population.

Unfortunately, that will require (as I have adamantly stated in my lectures at San Jose State University - at both the Graduate and Undergraduate Criminal Justice classes) a "top-down scrub" of CDC to rid itself of "old attitudes" and ideologies. And, in my opinion, CHOW would be one of the first to exit.

[Readers, to eliminate redundancy, I intentionally excluded some of my written material in this letter since it has been previously addressed in my book]

Incidentally, almost immediately following my termination, every parole agent in the San Jose area who wanted to be transferred to Sacramento was transferred! Coincidence? I think not!

Historically, San Jose has been the "training grounds" for parole agents who were later transferred to other locations, of choice.

Unfortunately, when I requested a transfer for "hardship" reasons, there were simply too many egos involved with zero compassion!

Again, was it merely coincidence that my replacement had already been selected from one of the institutions and was, in fact, working at my desk before the results of my Skelly hearing were announced? Again, I think not; especially, when CHOW made the sarcastic remark to me at the end of that hearing, "Stay home and take care of your wife!"

While I may be somewhat naive, Ms. Reno, please explain to me how a CDC manager, who has already initiated adverse action against an individual, is now expected to objectively hear that individual's comments and then decide its relevancy and the appropriateness of the punishment (that has already been decided)! What a joke! This makes a mockery of our entire administrative hearing system.

Please closely examine my SPB Number 36130 (attachment 20), as it relates to my Appeal from Dismissal. Do you believe, as I, that *the Stipulation for Settlement was in the best interest of the California Department of Corrections and certainly not the DeWitt family? This stipulation simply provided a "quick fix" for CDC and merely kept my home from foreclosure a few more months.*

Ms. Reno, if it is within your powers of authority, please make it possible that my case is heard in a court of law and that while I am waiting to be heard, that I receive all retroactive pay and allowances; and, that I be placed in an administrative leave of absence status, with pay, until my case is resolved. I do not believe that I need to go bankrupt while awaiting legal remedies.

I am depending on you, Ms. Reno, and I am confident that you will correct the injustice that my family and I have continued to suffer. We would certainly like our lives to return to some form of "normalcy."

Sincerely, Lonnie F. DeWitt

(Note: Copies of the entire package, that included 20 attachments, were sent to: Assembly Member Willard Murray; U.S. District Judge Lawrence K. Karlton; Congressman Robert Matsui;' Department of Fair Employment & Housing; U.S. Senators Diane Feinstein and Barbara Boxer; Chief Justice Malcolm Lucas and Johnnie Cochran, Jr.).

On December 15, 1995, I sent another (one-page) letter to Ms. Janet Reno stating that I had previously mailed her a letter; and that I was inquiring about the status of her reply.

This entire episode has truly been a monumental exercise in futility. The few responses that I received said absolutely nothing.

On May 20, 1996, I submitted the following letter to the Executive Officer of the California State Personnel Board (with courtesy copies to the California Court of Appeals, Sacramento Superior and Municipal Courts, California State Supreme Court and the California State Bar Association) expressing my dissatisfaction with the Administrative Law Judge's opening comments during my *so-called hearing*:

◆ ◆ ◆

Dear Sir:

On June 6, 1995, I appeared before Administrative Law Judge (ALJ) BARBARA BUNKER, along with my Attorney, RAYMOND A. BURRELL.

I was somewhat confused and dismayed by the conduct of the entire "hearing," as we did not go "on record" until approximately four hours later, when I was asked to verbally agree to a stipulation for settlement.

At the onset of my hearing, BUNKER advised that we would be, "off-record." (Both she and I had our tape recorders off). At that point, BUNKER asked me if I wanted to continue with the hearing or possibly settle the matter through mediation. I advised BUNKER that I did not want to negotiate and asked that we continue with the hearing.

BUNKER then stated, "If what I've read is true, it is likely that I will rule in favor of the State." I then replied that I was confident that my arguments would overwhelmingly convince the SPB that my actions did not warrant dismissal from state service and that the SPB would rule in my favor. BUNKER then commented that even if she did rule in my favor that there was no guarantee that I would receive any retroactive financial benefits.

BUNKER went on to say that CDC would appeal her decision and that it would take, "a couple of years" before it was resolved.

I then questioned BUNKER about the authority (or lack thereof) of the SPB regarding its decision if CDC were allowed the latitude to ignore that decision. BUNKER then stated that even if she did rule in my favor that she had no authority to state where I would be reassigned; adding that CDC would probably send me back to San Jose. I then stated that would be fine; as I simply wanted my job. I even reinforced my position when I jotted a note to my Attorney stating that the only thing I would agree to was that I be returned to my job as a Parole Agent-1!

BUNKER then asked that I leave the room while she, my attorney, the State's attorney and CURTIS JACKSON, my former supervisor, consulted. Finally, my attorney exited and asked me what would it take for me to settle. I then stated, "My job as a Parole Agent." My attorney stated that that was not possible, as CDC has made it clear that it did not want me back in any capacity! My attorney added that CDC would only, "find" another reason to terminate me if I remained in CDC.

This dialogue went on and on and, quite frankly, I felt that I had been browbeaten by both BUNKER and my own Attorney! I advised my attorney that I was experiencing extreme financial difficulty (as I had been without employment for seven months).

I felt very uncomfortable in that my attorney and I were outside the closed hearing room while BUNKER, the State's Attorney, and JACKSON remained inside for approximately thirty minutes.

Finally, with the insistence (not assistance) of BUNKER, my attorney convinced me that it would be in the, "best interest of all parties" concerned if I settled; and, by doing so, I would then be immediately eligible to seek further State employment.

Sir, I have grave concerns and serious cause to question the tactics employed by the ALJ at my hearing. For instance, is it either policy or procedure for:

- the ALJ to openly state a, "likely" decision prior to hearing arguments from both sides?
- the ALJ to disregard the comments of an appellant who has repeatedly stated, "no" to the ALJ's requests for settling the matter through mediation? (How many times must an appellant say, "No" for it to mean ,"No"?)
- the ALJ to initiate and orchestrate the stipulation for settlement against the objections of the appellant?
- the appellant to engage in "defensive arguments" with the ALJ while "off-record"?
- the ALJ t o discuss case issues with the State's Attorney and its representative without the presence of the appellant's Counsel?

I have been effectively blackballed from State Service through

Administrative Actions; and the sad reality is that I simply stopped and offered my assistance to a law enforcement agency, while off-duty.

While it is overwhelmingly recognized that the Department of Corrections had no jurisdiction in my off-duty involvement, nonetheless, the Department took illegal actions against me to terminate my employment, while claiming that I was, "on-duty." The Department obviously did not care that I was traveling home in my own personal vehicle and approximately 60 miles away from my Parole Office. My California Correctional Peace Officers Association (CCPOA), advised me that it could not represent me because my actions took place while "off-duty."

My Attorney failed to adequately represent me during my Administrative Hearing. In fact, I had asked my Attorney to either subpoena or contact several individuals who would offer credible testimony on my behalf. However, my Attorney advised me that it would only "piss off" the Administrative Law Judge by our having so many witnesses. Consequently, I had none!

I believe that my Peace Officer Bill of Rights were violated along with my Constitutional Rights. My case was not heard and I believe that I am entitled to a fair and impartial hearing.

Therefore, in the interest of justice, I respectfully request that my case be forwarded to the appropriate court for its calendar.

Sincerely, Lonnie F. DeWitt

Only after mailing my Second Request to the SPB did I receive the following response:

SPB #36130 - Lonnie F. DeWitt

This will acknowledge receipt of your letters of May 20, 1996, and June 17, 1996, concerning the State Personnel Board hearing on your appeal from dismissal which took place on June 6,1995, before Administrative Law Judge Barbara Bunker.

According to Board records, you entered into a settlement agreement on that date after participating in a settlement conference with Judge Bunker. This settlement provided, interalia, that the Department would withdraw the adverse action of dismissal; you would be paid the sum of $25,000.00 within 30 days of the settlement; and you would be placed on an unpaid leave of absence until November 30, 1995, at which time you would resign from your position. You were represented throughout the proceedings by legal counsel. You and your counsel agreed to the terms of the settlement on the record of the hearing. The Assistant Executive Officer of the Board approved the settlement on June 20, 1995, at which time the terms of the settlement became final and binding upon the parties (Gov. Code § 18681).

On August 7, 1995, your counsel wrote Judge Bunker advising that you wished to revoke the settlement because the Department was late forwarding the $25,000.00 check to you. On August 22, 1995, Judge Bunker wrote your counsel advising that the settlement had been approved by the Board and was final. It is our understanding that subsequent to this correspondence, you accepted the $25,000.00 settlement check, and the remaining terms of the settlement were carried out.

We have reviewed the concerns expressed in your letter of May 20, 1996, and have determined that Judge Bunker handled the matter appropriately. It is not uncommon for our Administrative Law Judges to assist the parties with settlement negotiations on the day of the hearing. You were represented by legal counsel throughout those negotiations. Your counsel agreed to, and indeed welcomed, Judge Bunker's participation in those negotiations. You subsequently agreed to the settlement terms that were negotiated and accepted the benefit of those terms. Under the above circumstances, the State Personnel Board has no jurisdiction to provide you with any further relief.

We regret that your experience with the State Personnel Board *process was not more positive. However, it is our view that your case was handled appropriately under the laws and rules governing the state civil service. Accordingly, we plan to take no further action on your case.*

(Signed) Philip E. Callis, Acting Chief, Administrative Law Judge

◆ ◆ ◆

It saddens and frightens me to think that other State employees, who sought only fairness and objectivity in past hearings, received less than they deserved from our *self-healing* **so-called** *administrative system of justice* were minorities are systematically ambushed.

In retrospect, I frequently wonder why my attorney did **not even bother** to question the ALJ's appearance of conflict or, possibly even, improprieties (given her opening and certainly inappropriate remarks).

For the State Personnel Board to conclude that my case was, "handled appropriately" leaves little doubt in my mind regarding the Board's views toward State minority employees.

It appears to me that the ALJ's absolute mandate was to deter me from going on record; thereby, preventing me from possibly airing some of CDC's dirty laundry. My attorney (willingly or not), aided in that deterrence that resulted in *a conspiracy of silence.* **Until now.**

The State Personnel Board, like CDC, is riveted with a history of *priors.* This Board has flaunted with numerous allegations of demanding its transcribers to falsify and alter official Board transcripts to favor the State's position.

This **S**tate **P**eckerwood **B**oard has repeatedly shown patience and overt tolerance when White State workers are accused of flagrant violations.

Consider, for instance, the incident at Corcoran State Prison that occurred on June 21, 1995. When inmates arrived at that institution from Calipatria State Prison, ten White correctional officers used chin holds on some of the Black inmates and proceeded to cut off the inmates' braided hair to, "look for contraband."

The Administrative Law Judge concluded that: "... They [White officers] did not know that it was unnecessary force. There was no procedure manual available, and that they had seen other guards use it at other times." What sheer nonsense! **"They did not know!"** I don't know about you but, the water is **Krystal Klear** to me.

Yet, this same Board continues to show contempt, intolerance and hostilities toward minority State employees by imposing the most severe administrative punishments possible. My dismissal (settlement) from State Service was simply a typical example of that **sabotaged** *Just Us* System where such harsh and bitter words like: *"Inexcusable neglect of duty"* and *"Willful disobedience"* were articulated to describe my *Good Samaritan gestures.*

The sad reality is that most (not all) White workers really don't need counsel, since they obviously have Administrative Law Judges and the CCPOA *representing* them and their *kombined best interests.*

Now, I ask, is it even possible for either a minority or other underrepresented groups to receive fair and impartial hearings? I see the klear formation of a totally disgusting and unacceptable pattern.

I have learned that **the one thing that is consistent within the California Department of Corrections is *inconsistency.*** Even my (former) CCPOA union representative, Mr. Mark Vinch, made the following observation:

> **"Ron Chow gives adverse actions where
> other Administrators give commendations!"**

It's truly sad to even think that our Great State - which has so much to offer that all of its people may fully benefit and prosper - has, instead, elected to drop the Urban Bomb. Now, we are all suffering the total consequences of its fallout We may well expect the residual effects of that bomb to be felt for years to come.

When does this, "high tech lynching" (as described by Supreme Court Justice Clarence Thomas) cease to exist? Does one really expect our Nation's continuing racial divisiveness to somehow, magically, self-adjust?

While I can truly understand and appreciate Ron Chow possibly having an acute psychological (and possibly even medical) *penis envy* condition, I simply cannot understand how our State Personnel Board could either allow or condone this continuing status quo and administrative white-balling of *any* State employee.

The State Personnel Board bit into the California Department of Corrections' *empty nest syndrome*; and consequently, I became the victim of a deliberate witch-hunt. I then became something more than merely a sacrificial lamb, since I wasn't simply sacrificed. I was **administratively sodomized** (without benefit of foreplay) by a cruel and insensitive system. I then became a victim of CDC's *Rule or Ruin, My Way or the Highway games*. I was more than its typical kill the messenger (Don't ask, don't tell) policy.

Unknowingly, I may have also become its Achilles heel! Because of my tenacity, perseverance and courage to address these hidden ills, the California Department of Corrections may now become a victim and succumb to its own poisoned arrow.

For all practical purposes, the California Department of Corrections and its co-conspirators, the State Personnel Board and the California Correctional Peace Officers' Association, may just as well dust off the old signs stating:

"We reserve the right to refuse service to anyone"

and, hang 'em high (the signs, not the people - I hope) for all to see.

President Clinton made the following statement in the January 1997 (Foreword) to the Blair House Papers:

◆ ◆ ◆

"But, there is a great deal more to do. We must give Americans the tools to make the most of their lives, to renew national confidence that we can solve our most difficult problems when we work together,

> **and to advance America's role as the
> world's strongest force for peace, freedom,
> and prosperity."**

◆◆◆

I, therefore, respectfully appeal to you, Mr. President, to swiftly and openly correct the injustices that I have addressed. By doing so, you may then help to, **"renew national confidence"** that *all* citizens must have in *our government.* My bipartisan challenge is also extended to every Local, City, County, Municipal, State and Federal lawmaker in the United States. **I want "Justice" - I refuse to be the beneficiary of CDC's *Just Us!***

My contempt for the California Department of Corrections because of the deliberate indifference that it continually offers minorities; and my *fiery commitment* to help stop that madness are most relevantly and eloquently expressed in the written quote by Mr. Mumia Abu-Jamal:

◆◆◆

"Contrary to popular belief, conventional wisdom would have one believe that it is insane to resist this, the mightiest of empires...But, what history really shows is that today's empire is tomorrow's ashes, that nothing lasts forever, and that to not resist is to acquiesce in your own oppression. The greatest form of sanity that anyone can exercise is to resist that force that is trying to repress, oppress, and fight down the human spirit."

(Mumia Abu-Jamal)

◆◆◆

The California Department of Corrections, with its inept managers, is in a rut. While it continues to build prisons for children, who are yet unborn, CDC also continues to shirk its inherent responsibilities as a progressive State organization. Truthfully, that Department has digressed to the era where de facto discriminatory practices and policies were *fashionably* blatant.

It's to no avail to have a tiger in one's tank with a jackass at the wheel. Yes, this self-made, mom and pop cartel is clearly suffering from *rutitis* while it *lacks* institutional *accountability*.

Unfortunately, for the California Department of Corrections, the difference between a **rut** and a **grave** is *depth!* A person (or an organization), with some effort, may fully recover from a rut. Sadly, however, a grave is final. It offers no promises of either a, *"good wood"* rebate or a *push-button resurrection*.

That sick and immature Child Development Center, that unethical State **Peckerwood** **Board** and that ***selectively helpful*** California Correctional **Peckerwood** **Officers'** Association - because of their evil nature - *will succumb* to their own combined madness, in *the Harvest of Life*, where each will (without fail) reap what it has sown!

"….ashes to ashes…dust to dust…."

Chapter Seventeen

Master of Illusions

ost Black Americans strongly believe that the swift application of *Justice* - as it applies to minorities - simply means, *"Just Us."* We earnestly believe that the blind, scarred and cataract eyes of *Justice* tend to open just long enough to observe a Black face before rendering *Just Us*. Police brutalities (*real* and *perceived*) against minorities, that are given little notice by the courts, will continue to perpetuate this innate distrust of our judicial system.

This *Just Us* concern is, therefore, unquestionably and understandably rife (and, possibly *even explosive*) within our Black communities.

We have long recognized that *legally blind* does not necessarily mean *totally blind*! **Justice**, itself, has become a casualty in this System that continues to treat minorities as inanimate objects - like plastic. CDC officials are then given carte blanche authority to bend, break, deface, destroy, trash, discard, displace, dispose and even recycle these *inanimate people*.

Sadly, many Americans (of all colors) have suffered severe and irreversible trauma caused by this very same - **Just Us** - a System that is **lawfully mandated to protect us.**

David Copperfield and Houdini would both have to take a back seat to the *real* Master of Illusions - the California Department of Corrections. CDC orchestrates a calligraphy of lies, trickery and deceit. This Department can pull a rabbit out of a hat where there was no rabbit and no hat.

This endless hoax of clever stunts that CDC masterminds may seem like magic but, the countless and twisted trails of shattered lives and broken spirits that this charade leaves behind is *no illusion*.

One need not visit a circus sideshow to see how ordinary people, like you and me, have become *environmental mutants* - because of CDC's demented perception of, *"fairness"* - while waiving its *selective magical wand*.

I had tried for seventeen months to effect a transfer to Sacramento; however, I was repeatedly told that, "transfers would not happen in the near future." Several San Jose parole agents were *magically transferred* to Sacramento where *magical vacancies* suddenly appeared; and the restricting administrative requirements *magically disappeared*. All of this occurred before the ink had dried on my dismissal action. Now, who 'ya gonna believe - the California Department of Corrections - or 'ya lying eyes?

These CDC officials are so consumed and preoccupied with hatred, greed, ignorance and insecurity that they *routinely prejudge* minority staff (and others who are not *iN tHE cAR*) and **axploit** them by casting that discriminating magical wand.

I will offer these officials a new sign to proudly sculpture and quickly add to their *pillars of shame*:

> **"If it ain't broke,
> don't just break it--
> --axploit it!"**

That could quite possibly become the California Department of Corrections' **motto for higher learning** as we prepare to enter into the 21st Century.

Based on my personal and professional observations, I would strongly urge the California Department of Corrections, the State of California and America, to focus on and correct the problems that we currently face in the 20th Century before we start *screwing up* a century that has yet arrived.

A great American educator, writer and professor, Dr. W.E.B. Dubois (1868-1963), once said:

♦♦♦

> **"The problem of the 20th Century,
> is the problem of the color line."**

♦♦♦

America, that "color line" problem still exists. If you can't see it, shame on you. Even the Honorable Thurgood Marshall, the first Black man appointed to the United States Supreme Court, declared during his retirement press conference on June 28, 1991, that:

♦♦♦

> **"I'm still not free."**

♦♦♦

On June 12, 1996, I sent a letter to the Parole & Community Services Division asking for some *administrative consideration* in light of my continued and apparent long-term unemployment:

◆ ◆ ◆

Dear Ms. Morales:

Since my leave of absence from Paroles as a Parole Agent-1 on September 14, 1994, I have been unable to lateral into another State position. As you are aware, most Divisions "hire from within."

My efforts in securing continued State employment, therefore, rest on one of two factors:

(1) That the Stipulation for Settlement be amended to allow me to lateral into a CDC position; or,

(2) That I be considered "surplus" to P&CSD and be placed on the SROA listing.

Please consider these options, as it has been nearly two years since my departure from my former San Jose Parole Office and, I simply want to "get on with my life" and provide adequate financial support to my family.

My option to lateral expires in September, therefore, I would very much appreciate an expedient and positive response.

Sincerely, Lonnie F. DeWitt

◆ ◆ ◆

Yes, I could very easily become a pimple on someone's *hiney* where I would irritate the hell out of him; but, he'll be too embarrassed to scratch it in public. To some, maybe that is what I've become - a pimple; a sore spot.

That System looked upon me as an annoying and worthless insect to which it could swat. CDC apparently exercised that option.

Hopefully, the California Department of Corrections, the State Personnel Board and the California Correctional Peace Officers Association are all hyperventilating from the hemorrhage that will likely be caused by the shock wave of this book.

Nonetheless, multiple systems like these are cooperatively responsible for the American Dream to find itself elusive; and in fact, gone awry for people of Color. Therefore, the responsibility to fix it is jointly shared. My advice to each of them would be to: **"Fix it, now!"**

After having been victimized and once again stung by **American Racism,** I can better appreciate the wisdom, bitterness and frustrations voiced by Malcom X when he said:

> **"I see America through the eyes of a victim.**
> **I don't see any America dream.**
> **I see an American nightmare."**
>
> **(Malcom X)**

I received the following response to my letter from Gene Suna, P&CSD Employee Relations Officer, in his letter dated July 11, 1996:

◆ ◆ ◆

Dear Mr. DeWitt:

The following is in response to your recent letter to Marsha Morales, Deputy Director, Parole and Community Services Division (P&CSD), regarding your inability to lateral into another State position. In your letter, you requested our consideration on two options to enhance your ability to lateral into another position. First, to amend the Stipulation for Settlement, approved by the State Personnel Board on June 20, 1995 or as a second option, to identify you as a surplus employee to the P&CSD and place you on the State Restriction of Appointments List.

After consideration of your request, we are not inclined to reopen this matter. We believe an equitable resolution was agreed upon by all the parties involved in the Stipulation For Settlement. In addition, as one of the terms of the stipulation, you agreed not to seek re-employment with the Department of Corrections. Therefore, in the best interest of the P&CSD, we will continue to abide by the terms of our settlement.

If you have any questions regarding this response, please feel free to contact me at (telephone number given).

Sincerely, Gene Suna

◆ ◆ ◆

I have been unable to obtain State employment for over two years and I am told that, *"an equitable solution was agreed upon."* **What absolute nonsense!**

It appears to me that CDC's perception of *equality* is severely demented which clearly amplifies my position that there is sufficient (documented) evidence that senses a powerful and suffocating stench (of solecisms) emitting from the Master of Illusions - the California Department of Corrections.

This stench (that has managed to even surpass the nauseating odor that lingered in the *Men's* restroom) is much too powerful even for the Master of Illusions to perform its disappearing acts.

Ron Chow *abruptly* retired. Apparently, Ron's baseball bat swung *both* ways. Now, one would think that an *intelligent* person would have known that: *"One who fondles with bats, gets splinters."* CJ received his *hard earned* promotion to pimp and selectively add even more parole agents to his *bootie call* roster.

Unconsciously, I began to view *CJ* with the same pity that I felt as a child toward my abusive and insensitive grandfather. The only difference was that I knew what *CJ* lacked! Now, *CJ*, where 'ya gonna run? Where 'ya gonna hide? You didn't want to be Black; and you clearly *can't* be White! I pity the fool.

The California Department of Corrections continues to violate human and civil rights. To me, that is an affront to human dignity and decency.

To this day, California Department of Corrections officials have failed to acknowledge their lack of jurisdictional prudence in the matter of the **"State of California vs. Lonnie F. DeWitt."** Of course, by doing so, they would openly expose this, *"fair and equitable"* illegal and shameful scam.

Every military veteran and, in fact, every decent American citizen should be enraged by the so-called, *"fair and equitable"* treatment and representation (or, lack thereof) that I and others have been (and are presently being) subjected by the California Department of Corrections, the California State Personnel Board and the California Correctional Peace Officers Association in their perverted and konkomitant roles.

Within the United States Armed Forces, there is a long-standing, time-honored and internationally recognized signal that demands the staffing of a country's flag - upside down - to warn others of impending danger or distress.

Therefore, concurrent with the initial publication of *iN tHE cAR*, I intend to display the American flag at my residence - upside down - to warn (or, possibly even remind) the California Department of Corrections and the American people that its minority citizens are in a dangerous state of distress! My book is simply the tip of the iceberg.

I applaud every citizen who has the courage to follow my lead until my grievance is satisfactorily resolved and publicly aired.

It's imperative that we muster a massive (grass-roots) *clean-up* effort - and demand a *changing of the guard* - to rid the California Department of Corrections of this opportunistic disease (prejudice) that has affected and infected its correctional staff.

The California Department of Corrections and the State Personnel Board must *both* be considered high-risk recipients of State and Federal funds. It is, therefore, imperative that we, the taxpayers of California and the good citizens of this Country, demand that funding to these two *entities* be immediately withheld pending a full investigation into my allegations.

I will openly agree that my stance on this issue will likely be an unpopular one; however, let's not forget that **I am the victim today; tomorrow, you may very well be.** If I must be further victimized to publicly address my concerns then, so be it.

I am appealing to the good citizens of California and to all Americans: **Let's stop the *crappy* rhetoric and become proactive.**

Let's put an end to **the California Department of Corrections' pitiful display of negligence, professional recklessness and axploitation** that it has consistently shown toward its minority staff, its minority inmates, its minority parolees and their families.

Let *US* become proactive and remain proactive. As a *United* team, we can remedy this fungus of decay and mucus that has penetrated and negatively impacted the heart of California's correctional system and the very soul of our society.

H-e-l-l-o, Californians, wake up! For those of you who *still* believe in CDC's *"fair and equitable"* solutions, I do not wish for your beliefs to become shattered and that one day you become one of its primary recipients.

To echo the words of the late great Ceasar Chavez:

◆ ◆ ◆

**"Once social change begins,
it cannot be reversed.
You cannot uneducate the person
who has learned to read.
You cannot humiliate the
person who feels pride.
You cannot oppress the people
who are not afraid anymore."**

(Ceasar Chavez)

In other words, the California Department of Corrections, State Personnel Board and California Correctional Peace Officers Association *cannot* and *will not* win this battle.

Just as the outcome of the demonic chess game has been predetermined, so has this outcome. In fact, the California Department of Corrections has *already lost*; yet, its managers are just too ignorant to recognize it.

CDC's demented peripheral vision simply would not permit it to fully recognize that to simply give up and *roll over* was clearly **never an option** for Lonnie DeWitt. I was determined not to become a nominee for CDC's freak of the week club. Their combined negative opinions of me would not become my reality.

That Department's discriminatory fantasies which culminate in its dispos-a-Black mentality, apparently gives comfort to that band of manly men who find themselves squatting to urinate while the womanly women stand tall and *erect* at the urinals.

What that triad has collectively done to me (and to others) is nothing short of a **vicious, well-calculated, racially motivated hate crime!**

Each member of that *triad* had so many other viable alternatives available; yet, they chose (either actively or through absentia) to make a decision that offered me absolutely no opportunity for recovery.

They *believed* that I would suffer permanent and irreversible financial and psychological paralysis. Yes, they mistakenly believed that their, *"fair and equitable"* decisions would ultimately leave me and my family *crippled* and forced to join their infamous sideshow - featuring *CDC's Mutant Families* - where people frequently pass by and stare. Some may even point and shout, "See, I told 'ya so!"

My singular question to that *Dynamic Trio* is quite simple:

"Why?"

God Bless America.

Chapter Eighteen

Beyond the Pain

s I desperately struggle to regain my mental and spiritual equilibrium, man's inhumanity to man continues to run rampant in psychological warfare. The California Department of Corrections may simply be an unwitting victim to this madness - - this giant demonic chess game. That Department may soon discover that it is an insignificant, worthless, and dispensable pawn.

A pawn that is valiantly but, terminally gasping for air - to prove its own power - while it daily suffocates those around it.

Sadly, I suspect that the outcome of this chess game (featuring black and white opposing forces) has already been predetermined; and there will be no winners. The demonic thought process (that unrelentingly plant seeds of fear, hatred, distrust, greed, envy and despair), continues to dominate our harmful and oftentimes fatal actions that we take against each other. Man's inhumanity to man continues.

My own personal, depressive state is nearly unbearable. My daily psychological pains are indescribable that I, alone, (with my family) am forced to endure.

Occasionally, a friend will call or drop by to offer me reassurance. Nonetheless, I have accepted this albatross to carry; and to be the brunt of personal humiliation, professional disgrace and financial turmoil.

I may, however, *continue* to be the source of some fears and concerns by some. I was, after all, labeled a, *"rogue cop"* (according to my attorney). *"A rogue cop."* I really don't know who gave me that label; however, the definition of a rogue is, "a dishonest and unprincipled person." Clearly, I did not fit into that picture. Another definition of *"rogue"* includes, "a variation from the standard" and a fierce and dangerous animal - an animal that cannot be controlled."

I freely admit that I *varied* greatly from CDC's *standards* in that I exercised integrity, honesty and compassion. It is also true that I would **not allow** that System to *control* me; however, it is grossly inaccurate for one to insinuate that I was, "out of control." Yes, I deviated from CDC's *standards* because I had the capacity to say, "Thank you," "Please" and "I apologize; I made a mistake."

What happened to me was, by all accounts, the height of chickenshit. I am, nonetheless, grateful to the California Department of Corrections in helping me to reestablish and reaffirm my priorities in this life (God, family, health and community).

As I watched the movie, "The O.J. Simpson Story," I heard a quote that I would like to share:

❖❖❖

♦♦♦
**"Fame is a vapor;
popularity is an accident;
money takes wings.
The only thing that
endures is character!"**
♦♦♦

Character - an ingredient that simply cannot be measured by either a manager's objective or subjective yardstick; yet, it is an essential component to other personal qualities (i.e., loyalty, honesty, integrity, etc.,) that clearly state who we are. In the final analysis, my friends, *character* **is** the "...only thing that endures..." that will stand the test of time.

I am reminded of a promise that I once made to the late Elder (Superintendent) Leon L. Ransom, True Holiness Church of God in Christ. When I fulfilled my promise, Elder Ransom looked me in the eyes and said, "You are an honorable man, Lonnie DeWitt."

At the time, I thought very little of those comments; however, as time passed, I began to gain a keener insight into my own character. Although I clearly took my own character for granted, I looked closely into the mirror; and I was most comfortable with the reflection that I saw.

Before celebrating his *homegoing* on September 16, 1996, Elder Ransom passed the *torch* to help guide us as we continue with our *journey of daily struggles*.

Life's experiences have taught me that, oftentimes, what appears to be convenient and quick to resolve isn't, necessarily, what's *right* or *best*.

In retrospect, as I peek back into the past, I clearly see *things* that I would have certainly done somewhat differently. Given that hindsight is 20/20, I can now use my experiences as a *lesson learned* and hopefully mature from those *very costly lessons* while helping others in the process.

Unlike the pessimist who sees difficulty in every opportunity, I am like the optimist who sees opportunity in every difficulty. I view this *storm* as simply just another *raging sea* that we must constantly face (especially minorities) in this transient life. However, unlike some, I refuse to become powerless in this daily struggle; and I refuse to be treated less than an equal, by any man.

I still have difficulty, to this day, fully accepting the fact that a convicted felon can be employed by the California Department of Corrections (in a non-peace officer position); however, I - who have committed no crime - cannot.

That's a repulsive and bitter pill to swallow; especially, given the years of honorable military service that I faithfully served and sacrificed for my Country. Even the most ultra-conservative (like Rush Limbaugh) would have *some* difficulty in fully accepting the totality of the negative actions that the California Department of Corrections took against me for merely *assisting* another law enforcement agency.

In many ways, CDC reminds me of the personal abuse and trauma that my siblings and I were repeatedly forced to endure at the hands of our grandfather. Because of his ignorance, hatred, and total lack of sensitivity, we all suffered. CDC has forced me to *continue suffering*.

Writing my book, *iN tHE cAR*, provided much needed therapy for me. I wrestled with many cruel and negative thoughts of *getting even* with some CDC officials who I believed helped ruin my career.

Instead, with the untiring support, love, understanding and patience shown by my wife, Ruthie (who seemed to sense and feel my severe pain and deep hurt), I channeled my negative energies to effect a more positive and desirable outcome.

I reasoned that it would be of no benefit to either me or my family if I were to do something *stupid* and spend the remainder of my life *behind the walls*.

Please believe me, if *thoughts* were a felony, I would be a notorious criminal confined in a maximum security prison, without any possibility of parole. Yes, even I - *Mr. Law Abiding Citizen, Mr. Well Disciplined Military Soldier* - nearly surrendered to **temptation** and to the succulent taste of **sweet revenge** as I grappled with many cruel, tasteless and evil thoughts of *getting even* with those maggots who caused me and my family this **totally unnecessary and certainly undeserved pain.**

I thank God (and others should too) that I had a very strong and solid religious foundation (my Rock) with which to rest. In God, I found a place where I could retreat with dignity despite the daily agonies that I was *criminally subjected* by the California Department of Corrections. I also thank God for the much needed support that my family offered.

God could not have sent me a better Angel - than Ruthie - who has always been there for me and with me.

It's ironic that I spent seventeen months *trying* to make myself available for my wife's medical and psychological needs following her hospitalization. Ruthie has now spent more than three years coping with and fully satisfying my own personal trauma.

I have gained a much deeper perspicacity of my inner-self, of life, and of people during my continuing years of unemployment.

On Sunday, April 21, 1996, while attending church services at St. Paul Missionary Baptist Church in Sacramento with my daughter, Shaneé, *something came over me* and I openly and bitterly wept. **God lookin' out!** I joined St. Paul's membership on that day (one week following my 28th wedding anniversary), as the church Pastor, Dr. Ephraim Williams, delivered God's message.

Before now, I had always taken pride in knowing that I had *broad shoulders* with which to carry my burdens and the burdens of others. However, this (emotional and financial) burden of mine became much to heavy for even me to bear. At that moment, I reached out and asked God to take away my pains and lift that awesome burden - that I had carried for so long - from my *(not-so-broad) shoulders*.

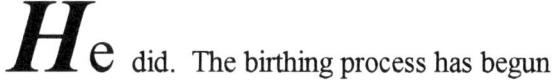

*H*e did. The birthing process has begun.

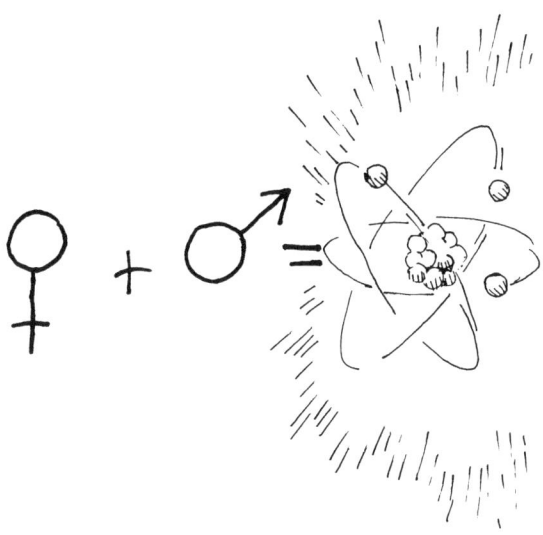

Chapter Nineteen

The Afterbirth

It's both physically and medically impossible for a full-term infant to be born without the mother experiencing some form of *afterbirth*. It's a natural biological consequence of childbirth.

Medical and scientific technologies have found that the *placenta* (or *afterbirth*) yields enormous quantities of viable everyday proteins and by-products that significantly contribute to humanity's quality of life, which would otherwise be unavailable. Pure energy.

These modern scientific/medical advances range from the use of *afterbirth* hormone injections to weight reduction products. Medical uses for the placenta have also been linked to providing possible cures for contagious diseases. *Placenta Plus®* - a revolutionary hair conditioner - is sold by the millions worldwide.

Why then, is it so difficult for us to believe that God can also use this *afterbirth* for **His** own glory? Just as **He** helped me to breathe life into the previously blank pages of this book, God also breathed life into my dead and withering nostrils during my *birthing process*. When my umbilical cord was severed, my eyes opened to a cruel and hateful world. Now, having been victimized and *forced* to swallow CDC's *bitter* (*Just Us*) *pill*, I can fully appreciate the wisdom of my Black ancestors and elders who use to say:

"We mourn the birth of a Black child and rejoice at his passing!"

If you don't understand that, just keep on living.

I have now grown beyond the birthing process and what you see is what you get - the final product - after the *birth* - the *rebirth* - the *afterbirth* - of **me**, "**Lonnie D**" - **pure Black Energy!**

Since my *afterbirth,* I have noticed one obvious *improvement.* I am now more tolerant to professional ignorance. I have learned that this form of *environmental mole* is contagious; therefore, one may have unsuspectingly become its victim and unwitting carrier. It's now time for that Child Development Center to receive its *baby shots* - to inoculate it from these man-made and other airborne germs.

Although I have never played chess, I am told that it is a very intriguing, challenging and skillful game of strategy. I have long recognized that *the best defense is a good offense.*

Therefore, since my *afterbirth* I have now taken a firm *offensive posture* in dealing with California Department of Corrections' officials. No longer will I allow them or anyone to place me in a position to *justify my existence.*

Conversely, the California Department of Corrections and its co-conspirators **must now** publicly justify their actions (and inactions) to the American people. I would certainly be interested in hearing CDC's **corroborated and scripted rationale** justifying its, *"fair and equitable"* decision.

It apparently took me nearly 50 years to *open my eyes* and rid myself of those rose-colored glasses. That is merely an observation and not a complaint. There are some of us who *stumble* throughout life spiritually blind while believing that we have 20/20 vision.

Yes, I still get angry; and yes, I still (mildly) cuss a little. My *original* character is still intact; and yes, I continue to give people the benefit of doubt in most instances. In short, I am still Lonnie. I'm just a *new and improved* (spiritual) *version,* as some advertisements would exclaim!

Now, please do not misunderstand me. My *afterbirth* did not come with the letters **s-u-c-k-e-r** stuck on my backside! Therefore, please do not expect *me* to turn the other cheek. I'm *not* the one. If someone *intentionally* causes *physical harm* to either my family, or to me, that person may as well auction the pink slip to his soul, 'cause his ass is mine! *Yes,* I said that! I guess that's all part of my being that *arrogant, smart-ass, you-know-what*! My *old school* doctrine demands that **"you have to bring some to get some!"** If you don't quite understand that, just keep on living.

Does that make me a *radical*? No. Does that make me a *revolutionary*? No. Does that make me either a *right-* or *left-wing extremist*? No. Does that make me a militia member? No. It simply makes me human. Just don't expect to *touch* me and anticipate a docile response. I **will** *reach out and touch you* back! I'm sure that you've heard the phrase, "My momma didn't raise no fool!" Well, that's exactly what I'm talkin' 'bout! (Just please ignore the double negative).

Regrettably, what is *radically normal* is the *highly suspect* manner in which the California Department of Corrections routinely operates while selectively dispensing its ***Just Us!***

The words of Thomas Mann (1875-1955), one of the world's greatest novelists and philosophical protesters of the 20th Century, do not merely reinforce my personal and professional stance against the *documented corruptness* within the California Department of Corrections but, his words closely mirror my own personal sentiments:

**"I am better suited to represent those
[positive] traditions than to become a
martyr for them; I am better fitted to
add a little to the gaiety of the world
than to foster conflict and hatred in it!"**

(Thomas Mann)

Similarly, I am spiritually and morally obligated to share my *irrepressible disgust* while exposing the *intolerable evil* that has clearly surfaced within the California Department of Corrections. I **still** patiently await a positive and lasting remedy.

America, I realize that it's important for you to *labe*l me; therefore, just label me as an **Arrogant, Smart-Ass, New World Order, You-Know-What!** Speaking of *labels*, let's now discuss the *Sins of CDC*.

All I ever wanted from the California Department of Corrections was to be fully accepted and appreciated for my God-given talents; and for CDC to *stop the game playing and call off the dogs*.

Once the dust settled and I was terminated *(forced to resign)* from State Service, all I wanted was the *opportunity* to provide continued financial support to my family. I simply wanted my family and I to continue *existing* at the level in which we were previously accustomed. Obviously, **I expected too much.**

Remember the old shell game? That's right, CDC plays the shell game with a *new* twist. Under the first shell is **Just Us**. Under the second shell is **Just Us**. And, under the third shell is **Just Us**. Need I say more?

Writing my book was like piecing together a puzzle. It simply would not be complete without that *final piece*. To me, the *final piece* of the puzzle (my last chapter) could not be placed on the board until I was **absolutely confident** that the Deputy Director of Parole and Community Services Division was **personally involved with and fully aware of** my circumstances.

I had somehow convinced myself that it was *certainly possible* (though remote) that the Deputy Director was given false and misleading information in which to make an informed and objective decision. *My character* - in giving people the benefit of the doubt (unconditional positive regard) - *demanded* that I know the truth.

On November 8, 1996, I got that opportunity. My youngest son, Lonnie Jr., graduated from the Parole Agent Academy. He and I had previously discussed (at length) the many problems that I encountered with Regions I and II. I assured Lonnie Jr., that *his* Regional Administrator would, hopefully, breathe now and then and show some signs of *life* and *humanity*. Therefore, Lonnie would avoid similar problems that I now faced.

During the ceremony, the Deputy Director and the Assistant Deputy Director of Parole and Community Services Division both gave *beautiful* speeches. The Deputy spoke about "integrity," "character," "honesty," and "compassion." The Assistant Deputy spoke about parole agents being "assertive," "proactive," and "responsive."

After hearing both speeches, I just *knew* that they could *not* have possibly been fully aware of my circumstances. I seized the moment.

Immediately following the ceremony, I approached Marsha Morales (Deputy Director) and introduced myself. I asked if she were aware of my circumstances and she replied affirmatively. I then asked if it were a, "done deal" or if there were something that she and I could discuss and hopefully, mutually resolve. She gave me her card and said that she would, "be very happy to discuss" this matter with me and she thanked me for the manner in which I approached her on the subject.

At one point, during the composition of this exhausting *documentation (iN tHE cAR)*, I had actually considered *not* writing this book. I quickly learned that *I wasn't running nothin' here*! I had no options to take; no decisions to make. I wasn't in control; I wasn't even in charge. I wasn't even remotely aware that I *was on a mission*. Yes, I quickly discovered that I was merely **God's chosen instrument** that **He** used to further **His Kingdom**. I had no choice but, to **obey**!

Of course, I followed up with that *invitation* and I was eventually scheduled for a meeting with the Deputy Director and the Assistant Deputy Director on December 13, 1996. During that meeting I showed both parties several huge stacks of *rejected* employment applications that I had sent to State, County and other personnel offices seeking employment during the past two years.

At one point, Marsha asked me, "Do you believe that someone here is preventing you from getting a job?" My reply to her was, "I cannot, in all honesty, answer that. The one thing that I honestly know for sure is that I am unemployed!" I went on to say that I still viewed my actions in assisting the Tracy Police as being positive and not within purview of the Department's authority.

To help *illustrate* my love, compassion and respect for other peace officers, I told both parties that I would literally, "run across an interstate butt-necked if I felt that it would minimize the injury to, or save the life of, a fellow peace officer!" I further stated that I would be the one *down in the trenches* (**helping out**) while other citizens would be on the hill (at a safe distance) with their video cameras.

I thought the meeting was very positive (or, at least, that's what I chose to believe) and both parties stated that they would, "look into" the matter and inform me of their decision.

Little did I realize it but, at that point, neither party could have cared less if I had thwarted the assassination of a government leader! Their

iN tHE cAR

(combined) crippled, mangled and incapacitated mindset simply would not allow them to support any of my (positive) actions.

I can truly understand and empathize with CDC staff who are reluctant to *get involved* (either as private citizens or in an official capacity) because they, too, fear management's *objective analysis* of *fair and equitable* treatment.

While CDC officials somehow feel a reverent obligation to play *devil's advocate* when tormenting Black staff, and other minority groups that who are **not** *iN tHE cAR*, this self-anointed **Just Us** System continues to perpetuate that - all to real - *unleveled playing field*.

One day (soon, I hope) the California Department of Corrections will embrace a doctrine based on objectivity that will *include everyone* - irrespective of Color - and *exclude no one* while dispensing its Adverse Actions and resulting **Just Us** remedies.

I knew that my anguished courtship with the California Department of Corrections was finally over. My one-sided, five-year love affair had *officially* ended. My *disbelief* and *distrust* in that **Just Us** System were replaced with a bittersweet closure.

Three months following my December 13, 1996 meeting with the Deputy Director and Assistant Deputy Director of the Parole and Community Services Division, I followed up with this letter dated March 13, 1997. (I was *anxious* to receive their reply, as I *desperately* needed the last piece of the puzzle):

Dear Ms. Morales:

On December 13, 1996, I had an audience with you and the Assistant Deputy Director, Mr. Rolin Mukes. At that time, I asked that you both inquire into my "termination" from State Service (as a parole agent) and the negative, long-term consequences resulting from that decision.

As you may recall, I expressed my belief that my termination was unjust and I asked that you consider my return to State Service in my former position - as a Parole Agent-1. You both agreed to give this matter your personal attention and advise me of your decision.

At the time of our meeting, I had asked that you provide me with an expeditious response since I had been unemployed - and, unable to obtain employment in State Service - for over two years - as a result of my settlement.

Three months have now passed since my meeting with you and Mr. Mukes and as you know, I have yet to receive any communication (either written or oral) from either of you.

May I expect a reply soon?

Sincerely, Lonnie F. DeWitt

True to form and clearly within CDC's *character (*if you choose to call it that*)*, I received the following **sickly, rubber-stamped, "Just Us" script,** dated April 18, 1997, (more than four months following my meeting)*:*

Dear Mr. DeWitt:

The following is in response to your letter and to our meeting last December regarding your resignation from State service.

Subsequent to our meeting, I asked Rolin Mukes, Assistant Deputy Director, to review the circumstances surrounding your case. Following his review, we fully discussed the issues of your case and concurred with the previous decision. We firmly believe the settlement reached in your case was fair and equitable to both parties. Therefore, we respectfully decline your request for reinstatement to State service as a Parole Agent I.

I apologize for not providing this response earlier. If you have any questions, please feel free to contact Mr. Mukes at (telephone number given).

Sincerely, Marsha Morales, Deputy Director

iN tHE cAR

In presenting my oral presentation and following up in writing for a response, I felt that I would probably receive the, *"fair and equitable"* reply; however, I wanted to be **absolutely sure** that Marsha Morales was **personally involved with and fully aware** of my circumstances. Now, I will sleep better at night by my knowing that I gave her every opportunity to correct this obvious injustice and to simply *do the right thing*.

Mr. Mukes, on the other hand, was merely carpooling *iN tHE cAR*. However, the moment he became knowledgeable of all the circumstances and the resulting human tragedy, he became obligated to correct this injustice. Mr. Mukes also failed. Now, if they become casualties when my book explodes, I will still sleep well at night.

I am not a vindictive person by any means. This book simply had to be written and *I was on a mission* to write it. Fortunately, or unfortunately (depending upon one's perspective), some non-CDC people will also be hurt by this book. Again, we must *all* be held accountable for our personal actions and inactions.

My expectations for these two Departmental managers were quite possibly too high. I expected them to *objectively evaluate and decide*; but, they both fell considerably short.

I have been systematically violated, persecuted and administratively victimized by this *surrogate,* ***Just Us*** System that has the audacity to persistently regurgitate and chant its scripted commentary:

"…fair and equitable…"

"…fair and equitable…"

"…fair and equitable…"

My words of advice to that Child Development Center:

❖❖❖

"Practice what you speech!"
(Someone just may be listening)

❖❖❖

I pray that I do not become overly consumed with cynicism - the *moral fiber* of CDC's sick, virtual reality of in-breeding mannequins - which would distort my logic and cause me to think and act irrationally without benefit of compassion.

Even now, when I hear a speech with the words, "moral fiber," I unconsciously - and with *some cynicism*, to be sure - develop a mental image of a new brand of cereal. Those words will no longer have the same positive impact that they once had when I wore my rose-colored glasses.

Now, just because my manuscript was mailed to the United States Copyright Office on September 23, 1996, (three months *before* my meeting with Paroles officials) and the effective date of registration was recorded on October 4, 1996, does not mean that I *planned* the outcome of this entire scenario, does it? Of course not.

I could not have possibly planned this, since planning requires *analytical skills* - skills that *CJ* made it quite clear and as a matter of public record - that I failed to exhibit.

I offer no apologies. I, too, will face the closest of scrutiny as the opposing forces attempt to challenge my credibility and discredit me. Nonetheless, I am mentally and spiritually anticipating that challenge.

My words of advice to those negative forces would include: "Plan to wake up early in the morning; go to bed late at night; and pack a lunch because you are going to have a full-time job on your hands (in trying to discredit me)." They may find that I am above intimidation. It's just not that kind of a party. They'll also learn *not* to **go messin' 'round with God's children!** So, if you're a party pooper - **stay home!**

I am quite possibly at the *crossroads* of my life; and I am personally *fed up* with **f-e-d** (**f**ear, **e**nvy, and **d**istrust). Aren't you? I'm talking about the psychologically divisive **f-e-d** that William (Willie) Lynch (a White slave owner) addressed on the banks of the James River in 1712, as a *blueprint* for America to, *"control"* its slaves.

Lynch predicted that "…..it (**f**ear, **e**nvy, and **d**istrust) will become self-refueling for hundreds or maybe even thousands of years….."

Yes, that *foolproof plan* has served America well.

Every American ought to read the infamous **Willie Lynch Letter**. Some of you may be surprised to *discover why* you *act* the way you do. Now, why did I go there? Maybe, I had better leave that alone!

I am reminded of a Biblical passage which states:

"Where there is no vision, the people perish..."

(Proverbs 29:18)

While that passage is certainly true, I would cautiously advise, however, that:

"Vision, without action, is naught!"

(Lonnie F. DeWitt)

Let's get it together, my people.

One year has gone by since my *birthing process* began. Ruthie and I celebrated our 29th wedding anniversary on April 13, 1997. **To this day, I have still been unable to gain permanent employment. Something is seriously wrong with that picture, America!**

I love you, America; but, I am *very much* disappointed in you. Am I destined to spend my lifetime as an, "unhappy camper" on your shores?

Is it possible that the Honorable Minister Louis Farrakhan (Nation of Islam) holds the key - the answers - for Black America? In reference to the Million Man March), Minister Farrakhan said, *"...Here is a unique contribution that Blacks can make to the survival of this Nation .... [by] ....challenging America with the force of our unity and the power of our logic..."*

I simply don't know. I can only continue asking questions and seeking answers to the **truth**.

"As Salaam Aliakum"
(Peace Be Unto You)

Could it also be possible that the Reverend Jesse Jackson holds that *same key* - the answers - for Black America? In reference to the Sacramento, California "Save the Dream" march, the Reverend Jesse Jackson said, **"When the Lord said a storm was coming, He didn't tell Noah to take swimming lessons, He told him to build an ark ... we've got to build a structure."**

Am I destined to become part of that, "structure" - a bridge - to link those two powerful (Black) forces together to form the *Power of One*? If so, I humbly accept my destiny. I strongly suspect that the Kowardly occupants *iN tHE cAR* would much rather take that long overdue 666-mile, one-way detour than to *cross* (✞) that bridge!

Again, I simply don't know. I can only continue asking questions and seeking answers to the **truth**.

What I *do know* is that Black America has been sold a **bogus** *Bill of Goods* that just ain't workin'. To me, it is quite apparent that I do not have the right Komplexion to make the Konnection as I remain in *administrative exile*.

I will once again capture the spirit, compassion and wisdom of Thomas Mann in his written prayer:

"God help our darkened and desecrated country and teach it to make its peace with the world and with itself!"

(Thomas Mann)

Please forgive me for venting. I'm simply, "tired of being tired." I may *seem* non-Christian-like. I really don't know, though, because I'm still not use to this *afterbirth* thing.

I realize that my book is somewhat *rough around the edges;* however, I never claimed to be a writer. But, I do know how to read; and I *clearly* know how to **document.** It's my *documentation* of a real life, *sicker than sick American tragedy.* *iN tHE cAR* is written from the heart; it's *my story.*

Someday, America, I *may* forgive….but, I'll *never* forget!

My two older brothers, James and John, are *still* my heroes. I hope that they both approve of *iN tHE cAR* and the aggressive stance that I have taken. The love, respect, guidance and unconditional positive regard that James and John have continuously shown me, since our El Centro childhood days, have not gone unnoticed. My most deepest gratitude and appreciation are mere reflections of the reciprocating love in my having two older brothers who really cared.

Thanks, James and John. **"Good lookin' out!"**

Like most people, I enjoy a *good* joke. I even enjoy being the occasional subject of a *good* joke. When a *good* joke, however, becomes malicious, I take strong exception; regardless of who happens to be the subject. To that end, I will neither waiver nor retreat.

I am spiritually and philosophically committed to integrity and my beliefs in the *Power of One,* which demand that:

◆ ◆ ◆

**"Once the line is drawn in the sand,
I will not straddle!"**

(Lonnie F. DeWitt)

◆ ◆ ◆

**No, America, freedom is *NOT* really free.
*But, I finally am.***

Still, I won't be able to rest, until I hear Him say:

"Well done, thou good and faithful servant:
thou hath been faithful over a few things,
I will make thee ruler over many things:
enter thou into the joy of thy Lord."
(Matthews 25:21)

The Afterbirth continues....
....the battle continues....
....and I will continue
to seek my *rightful* place
in the sun!

"Deus Vobiscum"
(God be with you)

Ode to The Dynamic Trio

Like so many times before,
this *Dynamic Trio*
went too far.

While chanting,
"fair and equitable" solution,
their combined hot air merely
contributed to California's pollution.

While perpetuating
fear, envy and distrust,
this *Dynamic Trio*
discriminately dealt, ***"Just Us."***

The games that they played
on that unleveled playing field,
literally forced many good players
to either fight or yield.

It's truly unfortunate that
their, *"good wood"* mentalities
forced my God's hands to
bring 'em back into reality.

They almost got away
with their sins once again,
had it not been for the
perseverance of a
real **Black man**.

The moral of this
sick and twisted tale
is to forewarn this *Dynamic Trio*
that their ghostly *reign of terror*
is about to end;

they're only "666" miles to hell!

The Joke is on You - Three

Lonnie Faustino DeWitt

ABOUT THE AUTHOR

Lonnie Faustino DeWitt was born in El Centro, California on January 4, 1947 to James and Alice DeWitt. Upon the death of his mother in 1957, Lonnie moved to San Francisco, California where he graduated from Polytechnic High School in 1965 as the Class Valedictorian.

Lonnie holds an Associate of Science Degree in Business, at Victor Valley College; an Associate of Science Degree in Administration, with the Community College of the Air Force; and, an Associate of Arts Degree and Bachelor of Science Degree in Business Management, with the University of Maryland. In addition, Lonnie has also accumulated twelve semester hours toward a Master of Science Degree in Systems Management with Golden Gate University.

Lonnie enlisted into the United States Air Force in 1965 and was subsequently deployed to the Republic of South Vietnam, where he served from 1966 to 1967. It was in the Spring of 1967, while stationed at DaNang Air Base, Vietnam, where Lonnie wrote his poem, *"Vietnam - Mirrored Visions."* Lonnie is now a highly decorated, retired Air Force veteran of over twenty-three years.

Lonnie is married to the former Ruthie Louise Thorn of Shreveport, Louisiana. They are the proud parents of two young men, Kenslo Gary and Lonnie Faustino, Jr., and a lovely daughter, Shaneé Faustina.

After traveling worldwide, Lonnie, Ruthie and Shaneé now reside in Sacramento, California.